MALCOLM X:
SPEECHES AT HARVARD

MALCOLM X:
SPEECHES AT HARVARD

Edited, with an Introduction and New Preface,
by Archie Epps

PARAGON HOUSE
NEW YORK

First Paragon House edition, 1991

Published in the United States by
Paragon House
90 Fifth Avenue
New York, N.Y. 10011

Reprinted by arrangement with William Morrow & Co., Inc.

10 9 8 7 6 5 4 3

Grateful acknowledgment is made to:

Edward B. Marks Music Corporation for permission to quote from "Strange
Fruit." Copyright Edward B. Marks Music Corporation. Used by
permission.
Horizon Press, New York, and Cassell and Company Ltd., London, for
permission to quote from *Blues Fell This Morning: The Meaning of the Blues* by
Paul Oliver. Copyright 1960.
Doubleday & Company, Inc., New York, and Methuen & Company, Ltd.,
London, for permission to quote from *Shakespeare Our Contemporary* by Jan
Kott, translated by Boleslaw Taborski. Copyright © 1964 by Panstwowe
Wydawnictwo Naukowe. Copyright © 1964, 1965, 1966 by Doubleday &
Company, Inc.
Grove Press for permission to quote from *The Autobiography of Malcolm X.*
Copyright © 1964 by Alex Haley and Malcolm X. Copyright © 1965 by
Alex Haley and Betty Shabazz. All rights reserved.
Merit Publishers for permission to quote from *Malcolm X Speaks.* Copyright ©
1965 by Merit Publishers and Betty Shabazz. All rights reserved.
Leverett House, Harvard University, for permission to include The Leverett
House Forum of March 18, 1964.
The Harvard Law School Forum for permission to include the Harvard Law
School Forums of March 24, 1961, and December 16, 1964.

Library of Congress Cataloging-in-Publication Data

X, Malcolm, 1925–1965.
    [Speeches of Malcolm X at Harvard]
    Malcolm X : speeches at Harvard / edited, with a new preface, by
Archie Epps. — 1st Paragon House ed.
        p.   cm.
    Previously published as: The speeches of Malcolm X at Harvard. New York :
Morrow, 1968.
    ISBN 1-55778-479-5 (paper)
    1. X, Malcolm, 1925–1965.   2. United States—Race relations.
3. Black Muslims.   4. Afro-Americans—Civil rights.   I. Epps,
Archie C.   II. Title.
BP223.Z8L5799   1991
320.5'4—dc20   91-22554
                                                        CIP

Manufactured in the United States of America

For
John Usher Monro

EDITOR'S NOTE

You have in hand a book about one of the most powerful black voices of the twentieth century. It is a second edition of a book first published in 1968. This present edition contains a new preface that tries to comprehend the resurgence of interest in Malcolm X. It includes an extended introductory essay, "The Paradoxes of Malcolm X," which is a study of his language and the unique logic of his thoughts.

The original material retains the name Negro, then in vogue, although Malcolm X often referred to the "so-called Negro," suggesting that the current name had not been discovered. Today we use black and African-American interchangeably, with the latter becoming more accepted, both within and outside the group.

Archie Epps
Cambridge, Massachusetts
November 1992

CONTENTS

My parts, my title, and my perfect soul
Shall manifest me rightly.

(Othello, I. 2*)*

Are there no stones in heaven
But what serves for the thunder?

(Othello, V. 2*)*

I felt as though something in
Nature had failed, like the sun, or the stars.

The Autobiography of Malcolm X[1]

PREFACE

Malcolm X and His Legacy

There has been a resurgence of interest, especially among the young, in the life and times of Malcolm X. The sources of this development are like undercurrents at sea, carrying to the surface his special brand of black nationalism.

Some argue that toward the end of his life Malcolm X's views were converging with those of Martin Luther King. Others say that he remains to this day the only authentic voice of America's black underclass—momentarily silent but waiting, full of anger, for the right moment to erupt.

Malcolm X is the great puzzle of the civil rights era, perhaps because his achievement was the most important: the "inner emancipation" of the black people. To achieve this breakthrough, he told his fellow blacks how slavery still defined the relationship between them and the whites. Unlike his predecessors, Marcus Garvey and Elijah Mohammed and the back-to-Africa movements, he never shied away from claiming for blacks the right to seek retribution for the way white Americans had treated them. You may recall the Mike Wallace television special *The Hate That Hate Produced*, which told the story of Malcolm X and his emergence as one of the most powerful and disturbing black voices of the twentieth century.

I was challenged to attempt this inquiry into Malcolm X's life by Eric Hobsbawm's book, *Primitive Rebels*, a study of radical leaders in peasant areas and urban centers. He has the following to say about the seemingly irrational and undisciplined revolutions in our times:

It is not always easy to recognize the rational political core within millenarian movements, for their very lack of sophistication and of an effective revolutionary strategy and tactics makes them push the logic of the revolutionary position to the point of absurdity or paradox.... Without wishing to make [the movement] appear more sensible and less extraordinary than it often is, it is advisable for the historian to appreciate the logic, and even the realism—if the word can be used in this context—which moves them, for revolutionary movements are difficult to understand otherwise.[1]

I have concentrated mostly on Malcolm X's language and ideas to get at the logic of the way he presented the black predicament in America. Malcolm X often conceals his real thoughts behind ambiguous imagery, using fiery rhetoric to make his case. Malcolm X's hyperbole is precisely what Hobsbawm had in mind. Its excesses sacrifice logic for metaphor in order to give graphic portrayal to the sometimes cruel interaction that occurs between blacks and whites in America. The terrible stamp of racial conflict is what gives shape and definition to his extravagant expressions.

Why was I drawn to the subject of Malcolm X? It was because I could never lose sight of the great cost that racial strife exacts from human dignity. If white people can only bring themselves to understand why Malcolm X was so angry at them and at the craven blacks he thought were their stooges, then maybe they will learn to respect the black people with whom they share this country. Malcolm X seemed to me to be haunted by his anger—driven, even captured by it. He liked to call himself the "angriest Negro in America." I would not wish his state of mind on any human being. I tried to describe in my Introduction what happens to a man who saw the world through the spiritual darkness we experience when we allow racial animosity to rule our lives.

But there were other, more personal, reasons why this subject was important to me. First, I wanted to make my contribution to the achievement of black equality from the position of privilege that I enjoyed. Maybe I could use the scholar's craft to shed light on a personality whom so many in the establishment feared or disdained. Perhaps an honest evaluation of Malcolm X and his ideas would strip American society to the bone, revealing a national ethos.

---

[1] E.J. Hobsbawm, *Primitive Rebels*. New York: Norton Library Edition, 1965, pp. 55-60.

Second, a first book, as this was, is usually autobiographical: One seeks to grapple with issues of personal identity and the meaning of life in the passionate days of youth. Like every other American black, the issue of identity was central to my experience during the civil rights movement. I was committed to racial integration, but I knew that some American blacks were being drawn to the black nationalist banner and its separatist message that had been carried so persistently through the years. Could we, through the voice of Malcolm X, understand the origins of that movement?

Third, I had known Malcolm X. We met in Boston in the early 1960's, just before the publication of C. Eric Lincoln's *Black Muslims in America*. We met at lunch and he chided me impishly for putting cream in my coffee (mixing white and black). It seemed a ridiculous observation on his part, and the conversation that ensued was full of such remarks. He took full advantage of our time together to warn me of the perils of becoming what he derisively called a "professional Negro." He was a unique and angry spirit, and, setting aside some of his rhetorical excesses, he had something important to say to me. I attended his first speech at Harvard. He had packed the hall with his Black Muslim followers. He frightened and puzzled many of the students with his ominous talk of no longer turning the other cheek. From then on I followed his career in the media, and we met several more times at Harvard for long, discursive talks.

My introductory essay, "The Paradoxes of Malcolm X," is an attempt to understand his place in American life. I discuss his views on history, social change, and politics, and compare them to the issues in Shakespeare's political plays. (What does it mean to be a king, a subject, a citizen?) I want to help those who disagreed with Malcolm X to take him seriously, for he represented largely ignored but still important black points of view.

In an essay in the *Boston Globe*, Patricia Smith argues that "the slain revolutionary's fury finds new life in disillusioned blacks.... A quarter-century after his death," she writes, "Malcolm X is again finding life in the people he sought to reach. Youths are sporting sweatshirts with his message; conferences analyzing the black revolutionary's teachings are drawing unprecedented numbers."[2]

Smith also quotes actor Ossie Davis: "The time is ripe for a resurrection of the man's fury. Some of us observed that Martin Luther King and the passage of civil rights had solved the problem of integration. Now that that glorious concept has turned out not to be the sweet chariot we thought, we're grasping for alternatives. Young people are beginning to ask, 'Hell, what happened?'"[3]

Another, perhaps more fundamental, reason for the resurgence of interest in Malcolm X is the unfinished business of the black liberation movement. Abdul Alkalimat, a State University of New York professor and author of *Malcolm X for Beginners*, told Patricia Smith about a conference on Malcolm X in New York that drew more than 2,500 people from 20 states and 15 countries.[4] He was not particularly surprised at the heavy turnout, and stated:

> Things have gotten progressively worse for black people in this country.... A small percentage of people have been able to gain access through the mainstream, but the vast majority have remained outside. The upper middle-class folks have been the heirs of Martin Luther King's legacy. But now the homeless, troubled youth, dropouts, and people in prisons constitute the constituency for the heirs and legacy of Malcolm X.[5]

Some say, according to Smith, that "it has taken 25 years for the grassroots to realize that Malcolm X is still in their midst."[6]

Malcolm X and Martin Luther King

One way to evaluate Malcolm X's legacy is to compare him with Martin Luther King. To do this, we must understand the origins and character of the black thrust for self-improvement,

---

[2]Patricia Smith, "The Malcolm X Factor: Slain revolutionary's fury finds new life in disillusioned blacks," *The Boston Globe*, February 20, 1991, p. 67.
[3]*Ibid.*, p. 67.
[4]*Ibid.*, p. 71.
[5]*Ibid.* p. 71.
[6]*Ibid.* p. 71.

from Booker T. Washington to Malcolm X, and the quest for constitutional standing from Frederick Douglas through W.E.B. DuBois to Martin Luther King. One of the most famous American observations ever made regarding race came from the pen of DuBois: "The problem of the Twentieth Century is the problem of the color line."[7] These words appear in his classic book, *The Souls of Black Folks*, a work first published in 1903 "to show the strange meaning of being black" in America at the dawn of a new century.[8]

DuBois believed that American blacks lived behind a veil. He described how his son was born behind that barrier, and how the almost immutable nature of the black experience would shape the boy's life.

Within the Veil was he born, said I; and there within shall he live—a Negro and a Negro's son. Holding in that little head the unbowed pride of a hunted race, clinging with that tiny dimpled hand to a hope not hopeless but unhopeful, and seeing with those bright wondering eyes that peer into my soul a land whose freedom is to us a mockery and whose liberty a lie. I saw the shadow of the Veil as it passed over my baby, I saw the cold city towering above the blood-red land. I held my face beside his little cheek, showed him the star-children and the twinkling lights as they began to flash, and stilled with an evensong the unvoiced terror of my life.[9]

The metaphor of the veil illustrated the hidden cover that encumbered the lives of DuBois and other black men and women in America. The veil conveniently concealed from white Americans the rage and desperation that ate up the existence of black people in a racially divided country. The tearing down of that veil saw the beginning of the civil rights movement of Martin Luther King and the black nationalist revolt of Malcolm X. Since this was not the first time that blacks had sought to improve their condition in America, it is important to have some understanding

---

[7]DuBois, W.E.B., *The Souls of Black Folk*. New York: Bantam Classics, 1989, p. 31 (forethought), and p. 10.
[8]*Ibid.* p. 31 (forethought).
[9]*Ibid*, p. 147

of the encounter between Martin Luther King and Malcolm X in order to understand the differences between them as well as the historic significance of Malcolm X's legacy.

There had always been two traditions of resistance against racism in black history, and they contained the origins of two movements that emerged in the 1950's. One was the tradition of peaceful protest and nonviolent civil disobedience for which Martin Luther King stood. Following this tradition, aggrieved parties sought to change some aspect of society while accepting the basic framework of the social order and the first principles of the nation. Martin Luther King had pledged his life to the principles of the Declaration of Independence and to the safeguards of the Constitution, and he urged his fellow Americans to rededicate themselves to them: the Declaration says that "all men are created equal"; the Constitution is the Charter of Liberty for all Americans. He never forgot, even if others did, that civil disobedience arose naturally from the American tradition of peaceful protest represented by Thoreau and others.

The other tradition of protest openly courted disunity and conflict, for it had as its goal total withdrawal from the larger society. Such a separation could be only temporary, while working to gain personal and political strength as an intermediate step on the road to racial equality and integration. But separatism could easily become an end in itself. Malcolm X and his teacher, Elijah Muhammad, believed, in theory anyway, that total separation from white society ought to be the ultimate goal of their black nationalist movement, the Nation of Islam.

It mattered a great deal what the leaders from both traditions said about the black situation. Their public utterances—mild or inflammatory—determined who their followers would be. Black men and women were drawn to these leaders because they needed to hear someone speak to their condition, especially when that condition was being determined by senseless race-based judgments of their own worth and by the arbitrary forms of oppression that accompany racial segregation and discrimination. The portrayals of black life by Martin Luther King and Malcolm X differed sharply and, for this and other reasons, they attracted different constituencies.

Martin King saw black history as the record of suffering, endurance, and change. It was also a history of courage, and a magnanimous exercise of restraint. King accepted Hegel's view of history as a dialectical process of progress and growth through suffering. But the dialectical idea for King, the notion of the struggle, was also taken over from Gandhi and Thoreau, especially from the latter's famous essay, "Civil Disobedience." King believed in struggle, in a kind of war, but a war, in Gandhi's words, "without violence." In King's view of history, the large mass of men and women must be led by an extraordinary leader, one with prophetic vision who derived his authority from religious values and from the people he presumed to lead.

King's views were in some ways similar to Robert Kennedy's: Both men dared to dream how things might be. "I have a dream," King said at the March on Washington in August 1963, "that one day the state of Alabama will be transformed into a situation where little black boys and black girls will be able to join with little white boys and white girls and walk together as sisters and brothers." History would also see a reestablishment of the original idea of the American Republic. "This will be the day," King continued, "when all of God's children will be able to sing with new meaning 'My country, 'tis of Thee, Sweet land of liberty, of Thee I sing. Land where my fathers died, land of the Pilgrim's pride, from every mountainside, let freedom ring.'"

Central to many of Martin Luther King's speeches were phrases taken from the everyday speech of the Patriot cause in the American War of Independence. As with the words that ended his famous speech at the March on Washington, "free at last," King sought to reclaim the old idea for a nation still divided by race as it had once been divided by conflicting ideological loyalties in the armed struggle against Great Britain.

The early period of the civil rights movement saw many far-reaching social and political changes. Perhaps the most important of them was the struggle to mobilize segments of the black community around some settled policy to improve the condition of black people in America. Malcolm X began this period as a member of a nationalist sect with only 400 members (its ranks had swelled to 40,000 by 1960). Martin Luther King began by speaking to an audience of 1,000 in the Dexter Avenue Baptist Church, Montgomery, Alabama, and ended this phase of his work in 1963 at the March on Washington, where he addressed 250,000.

The more one reads of the early period of King's public life, the more strikingly clear is the role of Christianity in his leadership and in the attitudes of his followers. King's religion drew heavily on what he saw as the analogous struggles of the Old Testament Israelites and black Americans. From this analogy, King and his followers derived their own notions of "a Moses," "a People," and "a Promised Land." Elijah Muhammad and Malcolm X also formulated a theology and political theory for the Nation of Islam within a biblical framework. Malcolm X's group included former members of the storefront churches, hustler groups, exconvicts and the more turbulent members of the black working class. Many believed that Malcolm X's political philosophy and the people drawn to it would inevitably lead to violence and to an even more intractable segregation of the races.

King succeeded dramatically in Montgomery with a bus boycott and in Birmingham, Alabama, in 1963 with mass demonstrations. He interpreted the Birmingham campaign in dramatic language:

In Birmingham we made a frontal attack upon the segregation and oppression of Negroes in Alabama. There, before the unbelieving eyes of millions of television viewers, and in the front pages of newspapers, we exposed the evil of bigotry in all its viciousness.

Predictably, the police in Birmingham resorted to brutality, using fire hoses and police dogs against black protestors. Newspapers and television showed the dramatic pictures of these tragic events that were shaming America throughout the world.

King believed that the Birmingham campaign was a turning point in the civil rights drive: It was no longer possible for men and women of conscience to remain uncommitted. Mindful of this change of thinking, we recall that President John F. Kennedy in June 1963 sent to Congress the strongest civil rights bill in the nation's history. Two months later, King led the famous March on Washington, an unforgettable event that brought black and white Americans together to hear King's magnificent "I have a dream" speech.

"I have no fear about the outcome of our struggle in Birmingham," King had said in April of that year, "even if our motives are presently misunderstood. We will reach the goal of freedom in Birmingham and all over the nation, because the goal of America is freedom. Abused and scorned though we may be, our destiny is tied up with the destiny of America.... We will win our freedom because the sacred heritage of our nation and the eternal will of God are embodied in our echoing demands."

Malcolm X was encouraged by what he saw as the combative nature of the Birmingham marchers, whose presence had signaled the entrance of a new breed of fearless blacks into the civil rights movement, a phenomenon that he hoped would turn the movement into an all-black revolution. He was referring to some of King's rearguard demonstrators and black spectators along the route of the march who had taunted the police and threatened violence. Malcolm X spoke their language and exemplified their political taste and style.

Unfortunately, Malcolm X was less than generous to his colleague in the struggle for black freedom. When asked what he thought of the dramatic events in Birmingham and King's leadership role in those events, he retorted: "Martin Luther King is a chump, not a champ."

One kind of ideology in the black community at the beginning of the King and Malcolm X era was characterized by a definition of civic life meant to counter ideas of racial inferiority and encourage race pride and civic improvement. The other kind of ideology was "grand ideology," a broadly stated description of the black's place among the races of the world. It recounted the great events of the past, the black empires of Africa, and the years of slavery, and claimed central place for a millennium in every black's thought and emotions. In one way or another, both Marcus Garvey and Elijah Muhammad espoused this ideology.

Malcolm X, in particular, insisted that an accurate description of black life in America had to turn a good many conventional ideas held by blacks on their heads. His *Autobiography*[10] and speeches contained new definitions of what it meant, in personal and political terms, to be black. Malcolm X had much to say about history in such passages. Emphasizing self-reliance, he spoke of the liberating points of view a black man should hold, the wisdom that could come from one's own life, and the struggles and the heritage of one's own race. At Harvard he said that "nobody teaches you always what you know how to do," Malcolm X said, "it just comes to you. That's what makes you [black people] dangerous. When you come to yourself, a whole lot of other things will start coming to you, and the [white man] knows it.... Anything that is done for us," he said, giving the theme of most of his speeches, "has to be done by us."

Malcolm X elaborated a doctrine of self-reliance and separatism. In contrast with Elijah Muhammad, he even downgraded the influence of religion and historical development in contributing to black progress. He believed that the group itself was his most secure source of power and advancement. His separatist program placed strict limitations on those who joined him in the ranks of true believers. A separatist had no choice but to embrace black purist doctrines and base his political stands on them. Malcolm's separatism was to divide blacks and create identity problems for those in predominantly white institutions, such as the universities.

Malcolm X and Politics

At the end of the introductory essay, I predicted that the next stage after Malcolm X, and for that matter, Martin Luther King, would be political in nature. That prediction came after comparing the assassination of Malcolm X to the destruction at the end of Hamlet. I had said:

---

[10]Malcolm X (with the assistance of Alex Haley), *The Autobiography of Malcolm X.* New York: Grove Books, 1964, p. 309.

It was likely that the dramatic leaders of the radical Negro cause would not secure the real, tangible progress the race had sought over a long, bleak history. The Negro situation required, as in *Hamlet*, that some other kind of leader come after a Hamlet. The prophet and rebel is always followed by the politician. As with Hamlet, so with Malcolm X, Stokely Carmichael, and H. Rap Brown. Hamlet is followed by Fortinbras. Fortinbras will propose to do public and political things

Fortinbras proposes no strategy of restraint. He is simply less weighed down by history, less likely to be burdened by the yoke that circumstances and history bestowed on Hamlet. Malcolm X needs to be followed by the same kind of leader. Fortinbras really supports a stoic and practical public policy; a politics of reconstruction—urgent and permanent. Denmark will no longer be a place of exile, but a seat of relevant, constructive power. The young may then inherit a new mood and history a new direction.

Malcolm X discussed the next stage of his pilgrimage in a now-famous speech entitled the "Bullet or the Ballot." He tried to stake out a role for himself as a leader of the civil rights movement. He thought, the black nationalist wing had an important contribution to make. Malcolm X believed blacks had to choose between violence and nonviolence.

His willingness to accord electoral politics a role was an important turning point for him. Circumstances, however, would prevent him from achieving his goal. It would be left to Jesse Jackson, Andrew Young, Hosea Williams, and a host of other black activists to cross the bridge to the political arena. Many black politicians like Jackson drew upon Malcolm X and Martin Luther King in the rhetoric that characterized this period. The themes of the "black is beautiful doctrine," the assertion of "black identity" and the self-reliance ethic were central to that rhetoric and gave it a distinction.

In his second Harvard appearance, at a Leverett House forum, Malcolm X discussed the political option. In so doing, he began to accept the civil rights agenda of the student-led movements and that of Martin Luther King's Southern Christian Leadership Conference. He foresaw that the strategic position of the blacks would be enhanced by the ballot. "A large Negro vote," he said, "would change the foreign policy as well as the domestic policy of this government." The achievement of the black vote was "the only valid approach toward revolutionizing American policy...." He went on in this speech to describe the intermediate steps toward achieving national impact. He proposed that blacks control the politics and economics in their own community. He emphasized the self-help doctrine espoused by the black nationalists who preceded him, such as Marcus Garvey. He saw no contradiction between separatist methods and the goals of the civil rights movement.

It was precisely in the realm of politics that Malcolm X sought to carve out a special place for a nationalist alternative, one that was at least dialectically linked with the then-activist civil rights movement. Certainly King's achievements for civil rights had been impressive. The year before, he had stood before an enormous crowd at the March on Washington and delivered one of the most stunning speeches in American history. The crowd that gathered to hear him on that sweltering August day was the last evidence of a powerful coalition of blacks and white liberals who would win the great voting rights and employment victories through the legislative process. The March on Washington was the movement's symbolic triumph. It signaled a new political presence that would reshape the political landscape in the years ahead. The new claimants within the black middle class were ready to reach out to a whole range of mostly white constituencies, including universities, financial institutions, political coalitions, and political parties. It remained for someone to speak for the black dispossessed and to warn that they did not share in the middle classes' newly won access. Malcolm X spoke for those who were left out.

No assessment of Malcolm X should neglect to recount his courage. In person, he was considerate, sometimes courtly in manner, and never abusive in debate. He also continued to grow and to allow his vision to expand. Before his final appearance at Harvard, he had completed his obligatory pilgrimage to Mecca, where he saw a mixture of races and colors. The experience transformed him. It reaffirmed his international outlook, and led him to conclude that the solution to the American blacks' problem was to view it in the context of the worldwide struggle for human rights. He sought to place this cause before the United Nations.

Alex Haley remembered Malcolm X's attempt to achieve a new role. "Shortly before he died, I heard one of the most anguished statements I ever heard from Malcolm. He said, 'They won't let me turn the corner; I'm caught in a trap.' He had just come back from Mecca impressed with the global Islamic perspective. He had written a letter saying, 'I have eaten from the same plate and drank from the same cup with fellow Muslims whose eyes were bluer than blue, skin whiter than white, and we were all the same brothers.' "[11] Had he been able to turn this corner, he would have been a powerful voice for the reconciliation of the races in America.

The Speeches of Malcolm X at Harvard

The second part of the book contains Malcolm X's Harvard Speeches. They were given at the University on three separate occasions, one in 1961 and two in 1964. The Harvard Law School Forum invited Malcolm X here in March 1961, and in December 1964. Leverett House at Harvard College invited him to address their Leverett House Forum in March, 1964.

The Harvard speeches represent three distinct phases of Malcolm X's life. The Black Muslims had just come to public notice in the last half of the 1950's, and Malcolm X's first Harvard speech aroused a great deal of interest at the University. It was largely devoted to explaining the religious doctrines of the Movement and the Black Muslim policy of racial separation. His second Harvard speech was on March 18, 1964, at the Leverett House Forum on the Negro Revolution. Malcolm X had just resigned from the Black Muslim movement and he was asked to say whether he would continue to work in civil rights and, if so, what strategy he would use. The final Harvard speech, on December 16, 1964, was given after Malcolm X had returned from an extensive trip to Africa, where he interviewed African leaders, and two months before his assassination.

Each time Malcolm X came to Harvard someone spoke in opposition at the same forum. These speakers took this controversial man seriously, although all of them did not agree with his solution to the black problem. As a result, also included are critical

---

[11]Patricia Smith, "The Malcolm X Factor," *The Boston Globe*, February 20, 1991, pp. 71.

appraisals of the Black Muslims, Malcolm X, and the black civil rights movement.

We do not have the complete record of Malcolm X's speeches at Harvard. The first speech is presented without the rebuttal by Walter Carrington and without the question and answer period, as I was unable to find the full tape of that session. The other speeches are complete. There were two rebuttal speeches at the Leverett House Forum. The first was given by Mr. James Q. Wilson, who was then Associate Professor of Government at Harvard, and the second by Mr. Martin Kilson, then Assistant Professor of Government, at Harvard. Mr. Kilson and Mr. Wilson became full professors of government at Harvard. Both were eminently qualified to speak on the black question. Mr. Wilson's study, *Negro Politics* (Glencoe, Illinois, 1960), remains one of the best. Mr. Kilson is a student of African and American black affairs. His *Political Change in a West African State* was published by Harvard University Press in 1966. I spoke opposite Malcolm X at his final Harvard appearance.

The method used in editing the speeches should be explained. Malcolm X was rather easy to edit. He usually arranged his ideas in natural paragraph form, with a topic sentence, a central organizing idea, and appropriate examples. There were of course problems in deciding what to leave out and what to rearrange; editing is a rather subjective business. What I tried to accomplish for the reader was a text of clarity that retained the actual order of words used by Malcolm X as well as his style and tone of speech. Malcolm X was an extraordinarily clear thinker with a penchant for synthesizing political and philosophical ideas. He was also superior in the art of rhetoric. I tried to retain his characteristic rhetorical habit of the aside statement by placing those phrases in parentheses.

I took two paragraphs out of order in the speeches; one in Malcolm X's final Harvard speech and one in my speech at the same forum. I discuss these changes and some of the omissions in footnotes.

A.C. Epps
Cambridge, Massachusetts
April, 1991

PART ONE

THE PARADOXES
OF MALCOLM X

I. PROPHETS

Earl Little and his son, Malcolm X, were both, in their generation, disciples of Negro prophets of race. The prophets predicted heavenly retribution against white Americans. The prophets dreamed of a new day for American Negroes, to be ushered in on the heels of the destruction of the whites. In order to bring about this day, Negroes were exhorted to separate themselves from the "sinful, hypocritical" whites. As the prophets thought of it, America was Egypt, who had enslaved the Negro, and such a sin could not go unpunished forever.

In actuality, the burden of carrying out retribution against the whites rested squarely on the backs of the small men in these movements, whose imagination often became distorted by their extreme notions of courage and who were sometimes lured to the brink of insanity by the discrepancy between reality and illusion, and between the rhetoric and actual deeds of the prophets. The prophets of race actually spent their time in speculation and prediction and, to quote Marx, "lost all understanding of the present in a passive glorification of the future that was in store for [their followers] and of the deeds [they] had *in petto* but which [they] merely did not want to carry out as yet."[3] Not waiting for the millennium, Earl and later his son, Malcolm Little, rushed into the prophets' holy war against the white Americans driven on by a fearless commitment to the cause. Their faith sustained them for awhile, but the careers of both men ended in confusion and tragedy. A part of the tragedy was that the history of these movements repeated itself. And the actors were cut from the same cloth. Earl Little was a disciple of the black nationalist Marcus Garvey. Malcolm Little became a disciple of the black nationalist Elijah Muhammad. Even after Malcolm X had resigned from the Black Muslim movement, he became a black nationalist leader in his turn, gathering zealous disciples around him. And the Harlem black nationalists became disciples of Malcolm X. At the very end of his autobiography, Malcolm X announced that he had indeed taken on the burden of leadership. He claimed, "I am also blessed with faithful followers who are, I believe, as dedicated to me as I once was to Mr. Elijah Muhammad."[4]

History seems always to repeat itself for the Negro people. In each generation, the Negro can always expect a new fierce leader to appear to raise the banner of freedom and lead the race out of captivity. The problem is, however, that the long line of radical Negro leaders—Marcus Garvey, Elijah Muhammad, Malcolm X—led the Negro in a circle. They taught the Negro that he was a slave brought from Africa. They promised the Negro that the "race" could be happy only if it returned in thought or deed to Africa, to its place of origin. They believed that America was not the Negroes' homeland. Malcolm X believed, for example, that the Negro was really in exile in America.

II. MALCOLM X's LIFE

The Negro radical Malcolm X was born Malcolm Little on May 19, 1925, the son of Louise and Earl Little of Omaha, Nebraska. Louise was a mulatto of Grenada, British West Indies, and Earl, a six-foot, very black Negro from

Reynolds, Georgia. Louise, a second wife, bore six children: Wilfred, Hilda, Philbert, Malcolm, Yvonne, and Reginald. There were three children by a first wife: Ella, Earl, and Mary. Little had migrated to the Middle West with his family from Philadelphia, Pennsylvania, to Milwaukee, Wisconsin, Omaha, Nebraska, and finally to Lansing, Michigan. Several months later the family was forced to move out of Lansing proper by the white supremacist Black Legion Society. The Society had set Little's house afire as punishment for his radical views on civil rights. Little built a four room house two miles out of town. Malcolm spent his childhood in this rural setting, surrounded by talk of "equal rights" and Marcus Garvey.

Earl Little was a free-lance "jackleg" or entrepreneurial Baptist preacher on Sundays and, during the week, an organizer for the black nationalist, Marcus Aurelius Garvey. Garvey's United Negro Improvement Association (1920) attracted an energetic tertiary elite[5] from the Negro working class; men such as Little, who were leaders of lower-middle-class Negro political and religious groups. They waited for real social mobility and based their politics on race pride. The most popular leaders harangued other Negroes with a romantic notion of the lost but glorious history of the race. The black nationalists said very little about the present and the future. It was the Negroes' past, the race's terrible history of suffering, and the lost glories of Africa that they dwelt on.

The UNIA was dealt a severe blow in 1925, when Garvey was imprisoned by the federal government for using the mails to defraud. But Little and other Garvey disciples shouldered the leadership of the fragmented movement. These men pursued faithfully the dreams of black glory that Garvey had promised his followers. Garvey believed he would return from prison one day to lead his movement. He exhorted his followers to look for him in the "whirlwind and in the storm." Little never lost faith in Garvey. He waited anxiously for Garvey's release. He arrogantly preached Garvey's doctrine of race pride for four years in Lansing, adding Reverend George Alexander McGuire's UNIA theology to his fundamentalistic sermons in 1926. McGuire urged Garveyites to forget the white gods. He predicted that soon Negro artists would supply a black Madonna and a black Christ for the proper training of Negro children.[6]

Malcolm's autobiography suggests that his father's life was interpreted in heroic terms to the children.[7] The day that Earl Little was murdered (sometime in 1931), for example, was seen as a day to be proud of. Louise Little had a premonition that her husband would not return home again. She and Earl had argued that morning. Earl Little had threatened to destroy an important source of family income, a domesticated rabbit, that he wanted for a meal. Louise Little had thought he was being unreasonable. Earl snatched the rabbit from its cage, ripped off its head with his bare hands, and then stormed out of the yard heading toward town. But before he was out of sight, Louise realized that the pendulum had swung too far within him; she called after him, "Early . . . Early," and he, realizing the same, quickly apologized for his anger by a hand signal: he turned and waved good-bye. To Louise Little this gesture was a final tender moment shared with her husband. To Malcolm it meant his father went to his death with the courage of a man, a notion that would become central in Malcolm X's ideology. I shall argue that this gesture contained an ironic mixture of bravado and independence.[8] As such, it proved, on the one hand, that Earl Little had succeeded in his work (in a way) by refusing to allow the Black Legion of Lansing to cow him into submission. Actually Little's gesture conveyed a fatalistic view of life characteristic of the great bulk of the Negro population; but a fatalism undergirded by a tenacity about Negro life chances. Negro fatalism was, of course, not so naïve as it may seem. It found justification in a realistic pessimism about Negro life chances in the 1920's. Along with other Negroes, Little thought himself a victim of the racist aspects of American society, and, as he saw it, of the historical and social forces set loose from slavery and segregation. He believed his destiny was predetermined. If he had lived in the city, he would have said he was trapped like an animal in the ghetto. Although Earl Little could claim a kind of prestige and independence as a Garvey disciple, he expected the worst of life—to fail, simply because he was a Negro. On the other hand, Earl Little was fiercely independent, and the success of his work in Lansing was not exclusively dependent on his accomplishments for the Garvey movement. The measurement of success could also be exclusively personal. Accordingly, by retaining race pride, Earl Little could believe he had made progress, that the white enemy was being routed. He could believe, to use the Negro folk idiom, that "he was somebody."

Earl Little actually believed in a paradox. He had not routed anyone. Instead, as we see him in Malcolm's eyes, he is asserting a pathetically irrelevant but real personal courage against overwhelming odds. The "respectable" Negroes of Lansing probably thought of him as a troublemaker. Earl Little was, in fact, hopelessly outnumbered and in real danger of being lynched in Lansing, as did happen in the end. Marx characterized Little's attitude perfectly. " . . . Weakness had taken refuge in a belief in miracles, fancied the enemy overcome when he was only conjured away in imagination. . . . "[9] As we shall see, Malcolm X possessed the same mixture of bravado and true independence of spirit. And as with his father, his life also ended with a pursuit of courage and in a premature death. When Malcolm X came, at last, to face his assassins, he almost relived his father's mood, gesture and all.

In his teens, at Mason Junior High School, Mason, Michigan, Malcolm was surrounded by white friends who believed he was born to succeed; to succeed, that is, at traditional Negro jobs. Although one of the most intelligent students, Malcolm was advised to become a carpenter. His ambition to become a lawyer was dismissed by Mr. Ostrowski, his English teacher and confidant, as totally unrealistic. The Ostrowski episode seems to mark the beginning of Malcolm's conscious hatred of whites. Ostrowski advised Malcolm that one of life's first needs was to be realistic. "Don't misunderstand me now," he said, "we all like you, you know that. But you've got to be realistic about being a nigger. A lawyer—that's no realistic goal for a nigger. You need to think about something you can be. You're good with your hands—making things. Everybody admires your carpentry shop work. Why don't you plan on carpentry? People like you as a person—you'd get all kinds of work."[10]

The Ostrowski episode is bitterly reported in Malcolm's autobiography. The word "nigger" is repeated twice in Ostrowski's part of the dialogue. Malcolm was "shocked." We have here the beginning of Malcolm's partial alienation from white society (which remained partial) and, at a deeper level, the merging of his conception of himself with Ostrowski's view of him. In another region of his mind, whites were hypocrites and sinister partners in a conspiracy to render him powerless, to beat him down, and to destroy him as they destroyed his father. In the face of Ostrowski's advice, Malcolm became silent, almost a deaf mute, slowly backing away from his white friends. A gesture of despair is suggested. There was a drawing inward, an admission of defeat, and we certainly hear no more of the law profession except in very wistful comments about it much later in Malcolm's life. Malcolm most likely admitted to himself then that he would not succeed in any way, not even as his father had succeeded. His friends and family wondered why he had changed; why he was silent around them. He refused to answer any questions about his change in attitude; silence was his new language, rendering him a mystery perhaps even to himself. He merely glared at everyone, transfixed by an unborn protest. Young Malcolm did not draw on his father's spirit here, but abruptly pursued an unfamiliar path into the hustler world of Roxbury, Massachusetts. He was to find that men in the hustler societies also lived betwixt and between the paradox of true independence of spirit and bravado.

In 1941 Malcolm went to live with a half sister in Roxbury, Massachusetts, a predominantly Negro section of Greater Boston. Ella Collins was an aspiring member of the new middle class that had migrated to Roxbury sometime after 1914. The poorest of this group had become the lower class of Lower Roxbury. The more successful, like Ella, accumulating one or more parcels of property, set out to win respectability among the lighter-skinned old Negro middle class. Characteristically, Ella wanted Malcolm to find a job on the Hill, where middle-class Negroes lived. She still lived at the foot of the Hill.

But Malcolm was more interested in the hustler society of Lower Roxbury. Malcolm's quick easy entrance into Roxbury hustler society really comes as a surprise. In fact, if one focuses on Ella, his most influential guardian, something quite different comes to mind. Ella Collins was quite ambivalent about Malcolm's hustler career. She was proud of her brother Earl's singing career in Roxbury night

clubs, but she wanted Malcolm to work a job on the Hill.
Ella retained a tolerance of hustler behavior but urged
the relatives she brought to Boston to make something of
themselves. When Malcolm brought home a "Hill girl,"
Ella was very pleased. She quickly and politely served
tea.[11]

A partial explanation of Ella's middle-class notions and
yet her tolerance of hustler life is found in her southern
conception of family allegiance. Ella preached a family
ideology that stressed solidarity and mutual aid. "We Littles
have to stick together,"[12] she had said, rallying Malcolm's
orphan brothers and sisters to her side during a visit to
Lansing. She would help Malcolm migrate to Roxbury a
year later. Ella had already helped other relatives migrate
to the North. "They, in their turn, had helped others,"[13]
Malcolm tells us. Ella's family ideology was inherently optimistic, helping to bind the family together as a corporate
unit, primarily to better cope with each relative's economic and personal insecurity. Ella literally stood at the
"way-station" waiting to help other members of the family
come North (to greater opportunity) or hustler relatives
leave the world of crime and take up a middle-class way
of life. Negro families of this sort relied heavily on this
ideology to survive urban life.

Consequently, Malcolm and Earl were not ostracized by
the family for being hustlers. On the contrary, this kind
of Negro family relied on the hustler relatives to reinforce
the swinging, tough, jiving life-style they used privately to
buttress themselves as Negroes in the face of the impersonal
city. What is more, the middle-class antagonism, characteristic of this group, and indeed, a more accurate reflection
of its political ideology, was more frankly expressed by the
more "low-down" hustler family members. I imagine that
the entire family, at weekend gatherings, eagerly joined in

the cathartic ritual of jokes about the pretentious old Negro middle-class, both loved and hated by the Little family.
Malcolm no doubt described for Ella and the other Littles
the sleep-in maid he had seen in Townsend Drugstore,
Roxbury, draped with a fur stole, who continually prefaced
her comments in proper Bostonese. "Ooh, my deah!"[14] she
would exclaim.

Malcolm did not really take seriously the more optimistic
aspects of the Little family ideology. He was attracted by
the bravado of the hustler society. He believed in himself
and depended solely on his own ability to make his way in
the world. As with such people, there is often a striking
lack of warmth in personal relationships, and the lack of
warmth can be found in Malcolm X's autobiography.
Throughout his adult life, Malcolm's relationships with
other males were tough and always contractual. It is only
in speaking of women (his mother, Ella, Sophia, a college
student, his wife) that Malcolm X shows a tender strain;
frequently confession of a personal fault is a part of the passages about these women in the autobiography. Other than
that, it was Malcolm against the world. In a subsequent
section, we shall see Malcolm X's toughness in full display
when he repudiates his mentally ill brother, Reginald, on
the orders of his cult leader, Elijah Muhammad.

A few months after his arrival in Roxbury, Malcolm X
secured a job as a shoeshine boy at the Roseland Ballroom
in the Back Bay, Boston, and a hustler career seemed
open to him. Malcolm was soon peddling narcotics. But
Roxbury was too small for him. In 1942, he took a job as
a railroad dining car porter working out of Roxbury and
Harlem, New York. He finally settled in Harlem and became involved in criminal activities (robbery, prostitution,
narcotics). Malcolm describes the rules of the Harlem
hustler society. "I was a true hustler, uneducated, unskilled

at anything honorable, and I considered myself nervy and
cunning enough to live by my wits, exploiting any prey.
A hustler knows that if he ever relaxes, if he ever slows
down, the other hungry, restless foxes, ferrets, wolves, and
vultures out there with him won't hesitate to make him
their prey."[15]

The hustler societies were fleeting social arrangements,
constantly threatened by fratricidal war which rendered
every man another's enemy. Malcolm soon learned to survive in the hustler's society. He lived up to his nickname
—the tough, urbane, devil-like Detroit Red. In Roxbury,
Malcolm was called Red, but in the more urban-conscious
New York, Red became Detroit Red. To the superstitious,
red-headed Negroes were literally sons of the Devil, quick-
tempered and capable of cruel violence. After a year in
Harlem, Malcolm was officially initiated into the hustler
society.

West Indian Archie of the notorious Forty Thieves
Gang performed Malcolm's initiation, and, from that moment, became his patron, sponsoring his entrance into the
inner circle of the society. Malcolm describes this curious
rite in this autobiography. West Indian Archie and other
hustlers "took a liking to me," he begins, "and knowing
that I still was green by their terms, soon began in a pater-
nal way to 'straighten Red out,' " as they put it. "One day,"
he explains, "when I brought his beer [in Small's Paradise],
West Indian Archie said, 'Red, hold still a minute.' He
went over me with one of those yellow tape measures and
jotted figures in his notebook. When I came to work the
next afternoon, one of the bartenders handed me a package.
It was an expensive, dark blue suit, conservatively cut. The
gift was thoughtful, and the message clear."[16] The message
was that Malcolm had been accepted into the society.

West Indian Archie's patronage of Malcolm had not
neutralized the fratricidal nature of the hustler society,

however. A year later, West Indian Archie, required to hand over $300 as numbers payment, thought Malcolm claimed it dishonestly. Moreover, he believed Malcolm had done this to challenge his standing in the society. Larger issues were at play here. Young hustlers often bluffed older hustlers to gain a more independent status. On the other side, older hustlers, to discourage competition, bullied young hustlers in order to keep them in their place or to force them to leave town. Characteristically, West Indian Archie challenged Malcolm to a duel.

Hustlers' duels were usually conducted in a public place (a street, a bar). Archie's and Malcolm's confrontation took place in the bar of La Mann-Cheri (146th Street and St. Nicholas). The showdown was aborted in a strange manner. West Indian Archie assumed the role of sage vividly describing the social forces that swirled about the two men. He lectured Malcolm on the fatalism of Negro life. "My life is over," he said. And then he predicted Malcolm's life was also over; "Kill me, you're lost anyway."[17] By Malcolm's account, neither man won the duel; both bluffed their way through it. And, indeed, no blow was struck by either man.

Malcolm depicts himself as the hero of this duel. In actuality, the burden of a hustler challenge lay on the younger man, and that Malcolm moved about stoically proved only that he refused to run. By custom, he had to strike the first blow. Yet he was afraid to go one step farther and force the issue. West Indian Archie was rendered without any courage at all. He seemed a figment of Malcolm's imagination—a fortune teller "seeming to read my mind," Malcolm said of him; a senile, defenseless old man speaking in childlike sentences: "I'm sixty. I'm an old man."[18] Malcolm's imagination conjured up a weak opponent through whom we can see his own fear of the constant dangers a hustler faced, and a curious introspective tendency revealed now and then in his autobiography and public speeches.

Indeed, the description of the duel, in the autobiography, was introduced by a strange romantic language. Malcolm shows us another side of his thought. Malcolm makes much of his favorite popular song, "You Don't Know What Love Is," using it as a song of courage. We are told that the famous blues singer, Billie Holiday, had sung the song for Malcolm (at the Onyx Club, New York) a few hours before his duel with West Indian Archie. It is a song of instruction bewailing the trials of life. In it the challenge of having to face dangerous situations is vividly portrayed. The image of the rejected lover is pivotal in most verses of the song, illustrating life as perpetual failure. Fatalism is even more strongly suggested in the lover's refusal to examine the past critically. The lover (Malcolm) seeks fame, but fame, like love, is elusive. And yet it was something to be pursued if only for the thrill of the chase. We get another glimpse of Malcolm's bravado.

> You don't know what love is,
> Until you've learned the meaning of the blues.
> Until you've loved a love you've had to lose,
> You don't know what love is.

Again:

> You don't know how love burns,
> Until you've kissed and had to pay the cost.
> Until you've flipped your heart and you have lost,
> You don't know what love is.

Two questions were asked of the lover:

> Do you know how a lost heart fears the thought
>   of reminiscing,
> And how lips that taste of tears lose their taste
>   for kissing.

And then two endurance trials were described:

> You don't know how hearts yearn
> For love that cannot live yet never dies.
> Until you've faced each dawn with sleepless eyes,
> You don't know what love is.[19]

The images of the song contrast sharply with the usual vocabulary of hustlers. Tough men do not "taste tears." Nor do they have hearts that "yearn for love." The lover here is in a world of very human emotions. The single witness to the lovers' embraces is nature—the dawn—who will not heckle but only salute their search for love. In the hustler real world, when you failed to act with courage, you heard the heckler's shout, "Go home, you're bluffing."

Applied to Malcolm, Billie Holiday's song revealed a region of his mind only spoken of through another person or a remote image. Malcolm was too preoccupied with proving himself a man to talk of these sentiments; to talk of love publicly would have been an admission of weakness. Billie Holiday was Malcolm's voice, saying aloud what he could not admit and dispensing courage no one thought he needed.

Malcolm returned to Roxbury two days after his showdown with West Indian Archie. He continued a life of crime there, forming his own house-robbing gang in 1945. He was arrested for robbery in February, 1946, and sent to Charlestown Prison, Charlestown, Massachusetts for seven years.

While in prison, Malcolm became a follower of Elijah Muhammad, the leader of a small urban prophet cult, with branches in Detroit, Michigan, Chicago, Illinois, and New York City. Malcolm and Elijah Muhammad communicated through the mails, and Malcolm's sister and brother visited him in prison, urging him to join Muhammad's cult. The relationship between the two men was similar in some respects to Malcolm's brief dependence on West Indian Archie in Harlem. The main difference, of course, was the religious dependence of a believer on a prophet. Harlem hustler society was thoroughly secular and encouraged individualism and competition among members for the spoils of crime. Elijah Muhammad insisted that Muslims believe in him "one hundred percent," as it was put. The cult was in actuality an autocratic brotherhood. Full authority was vested in Elijah Muhammad. In periods of crisis, the equality of the brotherhood gave way to Elijah Muhammad's policies. Indeed, this contradiction in conception would render Malcolm X the rival of Elijah Muhammad and force him out of the cult. This contradiction in the Black Muslim movement reflected other conflicting forces as well. It pitted Malcolm X's young hustler friends against Muhammad's older cult members. And, most importantly, it helped distinguish the more secular Black Muslims from the more religious.

Muhammad continually promised that the Black Muslims and the American Negro would surely reap the benefits of a righteous people someday. Muhammad commanded his followers to live according to the laws revealed to him by God; this would hasten God's assistance in the deliverance of the Negro people from bondage. No Muslim was permitted to smoke, drink, swear, carry a weapon, or eat certain foods, such as pork and corn bread. Cleanliness of the mind and body was essential. It was through observance of this moral code that Elijah Muhammad hoped to set an example and someday rehabilitate and free all of the Negro people.

The Islam of Elijah Muhammad was also given a political emphasis. It was a nationalistic religion. Muhammad encouraged the Negroes to stop being afraid of the white

man, to throw aside their slave behavior. To a Black Muslim, the white man was a "dog." In the Black Muslim view,
the American white man was reduced to the state of an
amoral beast. As a reflection of this attitude, the language
used by Black Muslims to describe the treatment American
Negroes had received by the whites and to propose how
the Negro should retaliate for this treatment is extremely
violent. It was this violent rhetoric that attracted Malcolm
X to the cult and, more importantly, gave his once unborn
protest against whites a new language. His career as a Black
Muslim minister gave him a platform. For his part, Malcolm X brought a genius for rhetoric, a fine intellect, and
the force of his personality to this new career.

Upon his release from prison in 1952, Malcolm Little
went directly to Detroit, Michigan, to meet Elijah Muhammad. Malcolm was made a formal member of the Nation of Islam that same year. He took the surname X in
place of his slave name Little. Malcolm X had soon advanced to assistant minister of Muhammad's Temple No. 1
in Detroit. In less than a decade, Malcolm X had increased
the cult's membership from four hundred in 1952 to forty
thousand in 1960. Malcolm X brought a large number of
Negro males into the cult. What is especially relevant is
that Malcolm X attracted a proportion of his first recruits
from the hustler society and its periphery: criminals, blues
singers, store-front church clergy, lay preachers, and ex-
convicts. Minister James 3X reported that more than 400
ex-convicts had joined the movement by 1958.[20]

Elijah Muhammad had organized this millenarian cult
around essentially archaic Negro religious themes. Muhammad was the savior come to lift the yoke of slavery
from the necks of the Negro masses. Black Muslim policy
called for the exaction of payment from the white government for the free Negro labor given during slavery. Mu-

hammad demanded specifically that the government give
the Black Muslims a state of their own. Negroes would
surely migrate to this state and live under Black Muslim
government. Muhammad thought this strategy would bring
about a new day for American Negroes. Black Muslims
exhorted Negroes to purify themselves; to become righteous in the sight of Allah, by joining the Black Muslim
movement and adhering to its essentially Puritan ethics.
America was no different from Egypt. Just as Moses had
led the Hebrews out of bondage so Muhammad would lead
the American Negro out of slavery. Muhammad prophe-
sized that Allah was going to destroy the white man in
America anyway by pestilence, disease, sin, or cosmic up-
heaval. On any count, therefore, Negroes should separate
themselves from the whites. Malcolm X became Elijah
Muhammad's most effective minister. Malcolm X preached
of Muhammad's nationalistic religion in Muslim temples
and public meetings in Negro communities across the
land. He spread a sense of alarm among the white population who feared the Black Muslims were exhorting Negroes to take up an anarchist strategy. Malcolm X said
nothing to allay white fear. He was determined to warn
the American Negro against the danger to personal freedom of continued subservience to the white man.

Malcolm X, with other young Black Muslim ministers,
ventured out into the cities, recruiting a "visible" and "in-
visible" Black Muslim following. They established six
temples between 1952 and 1957. These temples, in turn,
sponsored public dramas, public meetings, and commercial
bazaars (to demonstrate that self-help businesses could be
successful). The public meetings were attended by thousands of Negroes in every major city in the nation. The
1950's marked a period of spectacular expansion of the
movement, its activities, and influence.

By the end of [the decade] there were as many as sixty-nine temples or missions distributed throughout twenty-seven states extending from Massachusetts southward to Florida and westward to California. A comparatively small number of the buildings housing the temples or mosques were owned by the sect. Some of the Muslim groups met in rented quarters or . . . in the homes of members. Membership was estimated at 100,000. . . . In addition to the hard-core, tithe-paying members, there were many thousands of Negroes who secretly or openly admired the Islamites for their defiance of the white man and for the exemplary personal life to which they were pledged. The Black Muslims discarded to a great extent their policy of secrecy about their doctrines and activities. Rather they seemed to court publicity from the white man's media of communication. Elijah Muhammad held forth regularly on a network of radio stations[21] [which numbered thirty-six in 1962[22]].

The swift penetration of the Black Muslim movement into cities and in diverse geographical areas was quite impressive. Black Muslim radio broadcasts emanated from areas as diverse as Jackson, Mississippi; Houston, Texas; Los Angeles, California; Seattle-Tacoma, Washington; Phoenix, Arizona; Oklahoma City, Oklahoma; St. Louis, Missouri; Kansas City, Missouri; Chicago-Evanston, Illinois; Little Rock, Arkansas; Gary, Indiana; New York, New York; Newark, New Jersey; Pittsburgh, Pennsylvania; Providence, Rhode Island; and Boston, Massachusetts. Black Muslim temples were established in these same cities, in addition to Detroit, Michigan; Milwaukee, Wisconsin; Cincinnati and Cleveland, Ohio; Jersey City and Camden, New Jersey; New Haven and Bridgeport, Connecticut; and San Francisco, California. Black Muslim business enterprises also operated in most of these cities, with large concentrations in New York and Chicago. The annual income of the movement was estimated at $300,000 in 1959. The eight temples founded by Malcolm X in the East had completed payment of $38,570 to Central Headquarters at Chicago, Illinois, by February 26, 1960. The Harlem New York Temple (No. 7), Malcolm X's home base, contributed $23,250 alone, while Chicago's Temple No. 2, Elijah Muhammad's temple, contributed only $14,375.[23] The center of growth was concentrated in the East, and Malcolm X was the main catalyst of that growth.

Henceforth, Malcolm X, the major Black Muslim apologist and national minister from 1963, was a public figure for what remained of his life. In 1964 he was the second most sought-after speaker on college campuses. The first was the Republican Party nominee for President, Barry Goldwater. But Malcolm X was soon talking openly of how Chicago Muslim officials were trying to discredit his good reputation with Elijah Muhammad. He thought these officials were jealous of the influence he had developed within the Black Muslim movement and with the Negro population at large. He claimed he was not a threat to Muhammad but only a friend of the poor Negro who could not wait for the new heaven to descend from the sky. Early in 1963 he told the journalist Louis Lomax: "The Messenger has seen God. He was with Allah and was given divine patience with the devil. Well, sir, the rest of us Black Muslims have not seen God, we don't have this gift of divine patience with the devil. The younger Black Muslims want to see some action."[24]

A revolutionary speech delivered November 10, 1963, in Detroit, Michigan, signaled a serious difference of opinion and approach within the Black Muslim movement. I shall discuss this speech in some detail later in this essay.

On November 22, 1963, when Malcolm X referred to the assassination of President John Kennedy as "chickens coming home to roost," seeming to condone it, Elijah Muhammad suspended him from the movement for ninety days. Malcolm X remained under this suspension for more than three months. Gradually, Malcolm X came to interpret the suspension as an attempt to destroy his influence with the Negro people. He decided to break with Elijah Muhammad and the Black Muslim movement.

On March 12, 1964, Malcolm X read what he called his Declaration of Independence at a press conference at the Park-Sheraton Hotel, New York City. He said that he would continue a Muslim, but no longer as a member of the Black Muslim movement. His reasons had to do with the broader Negro struggle: "Because 1964 threatens to be a very explosive year on the racial front," he said in his Declaration,

and because I myself intend to be very active in every phase of the American Negro's struggle for *human rights* . . . , I have called this press conference . . . to clarify my own position in the struggle—especially in regard to politics and nonviolence. I still believe that Mr. Muhammad's analysis of the problem is the most realistic, and that his solution is the best one. This means, that I too believe the best solution is complete separation, with our people going back home, to our own African homeland. Mr. Muhammad's program . . . also contains what we could and should be doing to help solve many of our own problems while we are still here.

Malcolm X then presented the new program he would offer the Negro people:

I am going to organize and head a new mosque in New York City, known as the Muslim Mosque, Inc. This gives us a religious base and the spiritual force necessary to rid our people of the views that destroy the moral fiber of our community. Many of our people aren't religiously inclined, so the Muslim Mosque, Inc. will be organized in such manner to provide for the active participation of all Negroes in our political, economic, and social programs. . . . The political philosophy of black nationalism means we must control the politics and politicians of our community. They must no longer take orders from outside forces. We will organize and sweep out of office all Negro politicians who are puppets for the outside forces. Our accent will be upon youth: we need new ideas, new methods, new approaches. We are completely disenchanted with the old, adult, established politicians. We want to see some new faces —more militant faces.[25]

Whites could play a minimal role in Malcolm X's new organization. "The Muslim Mosque, Inc. will remain wide open for ideas and financial aid from all quarters. Whites can help us, but they can't join us. There can be no black-white unity until there is first some black unity."[26]

Malcolm X also put himself in opposition to Reverend Martin Luther King's nonviolent movement.

Concerning nonviolence: it is criminal to teach a man not to defend himself when he is the constant victim of brutal attacks. It is legal and lawful to own a shotgun or a rifle. We believe in obeying the law. In areas where our people are the constant victims of brutality, and the government seems unable or unwilling to protect them, we should form rifle clubs that can be used to defend our lives and our property in times of emergency, such as happened last year in Birmingham, Alabama; Plaquemine, Louisiana; Cambridge, Maryland; and Danville, Virginia. When our people are being bitten by dogs, they are within their rights to kill those dogs. We should be peaceful, law-abiding, but the time has come for the American Negro to fight back in self-defense whenever and wherever he is being unjustly and unlawfully attacked. If the government thinks I'm wrong for saying this, then let the government start doing its job.

For the moment it looked as though Malcolm X was to play a major political role for the Negro radical cause. He was embraced by radical Negro clergy, the student civil rights workers of the Student Non-violent Coordinating Committee and the Congress of Racial Equality, and the fledgling Mississippi Freedom Democratic Party. The Cleveland Chapter of CORE, for instance, sponsored a public meeting at the Cory Methodist Church and invited Malcolm X to address the Cleveland radicals. Malcolm X addressed the meeting on *The Bullet Or The Ballot*. On December 12, 1964, he participated in a HARYOU Act Forum in Harlem, New York. He spoke at a public rally December 20, at the William's Institutional CME Church in Harlem with Fannie Lou Hammer of the Mississippi Freedom Democratic Party, to raise money for the party. On February 4, 1964, Malcolm X had been invited to Selma, Alabama, by SNCC and said at a church rally that whites had better deal with Reverend King before they had to deal with him. Sometime in June, 1964, he had announced the formation of the Organization of Afro-American Unity. He had just returned from Africa on May 21, 1964, inspired by attempts at unity by African nations. But the new stance Malcolm X took, his political role, was really betwixt and between his old career as a Black Muslim minister and his new career as a civil rights leader and politician.

It was a role betwixt and between the religious and secular traditions of Negro life. Malcolm X's rhetoric had always embodied both these traditions. His early speeches as a Black Muslim minister were prime examples of this duality. E. Franklin Frazier characterized this duality in describing the sermons of Negro store-front preachers. "The speeches," Frazier observes, were "of a type to appeal to traditional ideas concerning hell and heaven and the imagery which the Negro has acquired from the Bible. In most of the 'store-front' churches, the Negro maintains his traditional beliefs and conceptions of God and the world and himself. On the other hand, in the new cults religion takes on the character of a nationalistic religion. Negroes could find salvation by discovering this national origin and refuse henceforth to be called 'Negroes, black folk, colored people, or Ethiopians . . . !' "[27] Frazier had hit upon a description and explanation of the Black Muslim movement and of Malcolm X and of an important source of their appeal to the Negro community. And yet, Malcolm X had introduced a novel ingredient into the Black Muslim approach: the ideology of the hustler society.

The hustler ideology was not religious. It tipped the ideological balance of the Black Muslim movement, instead, in a decidedly secular direction. The hustler ideology was at once cynical, fatalistic, and intuitively radical. The Negro criminal was the most alienated of the Negro group; and he often justified his criminal acts as "just compensation" due him from a society that had robbed the Negro of so much already. I have not invented the use of the word "robbed" in this context. In fact, Malcolm X justified the existence of the Black Muslims in identical terms: "A kidnapper, a robber, an enslaver, a lyncher," he said, "is just another common criminal in the sight of God, and criminal acts as such have been committed by your race on a mass scale for four hundred years against your twenty million so-called Negroes."[28] The Black Muslims existed to expose the crimes that white Americans had committed against Negro Americans. Malcolm X saw a radical solution to the Negro problem resulting from this role of the Muslims. In his early phase, the solution was religious in nature: the destruction of the whites by Allah. Malcolm X's post-Black Muslim phase found him advocating a political solution: anarchy. The criminal ethic of the hustler society was easily expressed in an anarchist strategy. The hustler saw every confrontation with an opponent as a test of courage and a call to violence. The first step in this strategy was for the Negro to realize who was really to blame for his oppression. Malcolm X used religious and secular language to give labels to the real villains. He wished to revolutionize the categories of moral judgment: "The American press made the murderers look like saints and the victims like criminals," he argued. "They made criminals look like victims and indeed the devil look like an angel and angels like the devil."[29]

The second step in Malcolm X's strategy was to call for a violent response by the Negro toward those who had oppressed him. A criminal should face a judge, who would say who was the criminal and the victim, and then he should face an executioner. At first, in the early period again, Malcolm X thought that God would be the executioner and punish the whites for their crimes: "America will reap the full fury of God's wrath for her crimes against our people . . ."[30] he warned. In a speech of the post-Black Muslim period, Malcolm X presented the Negro people as both judge and executioner of the whites. "We don't believe that Afro-Americans should be victims any longer. . . . We believe that bloodshed is a two-way street, that dying is a two-way street, that killing is a two-way street."[31]

Malcolm X's last days were marked by preoccupation with violence and death. This preoccupation brings us back to where we began in his life: to a mood of confusion and impending murder. It was claimed earlier in this essay that when Malcolm X came, at last, to face his assassins, he almost relived his father's mood, gesture and all. The *New York Times'*[32] account of his assassination bears this out. Malcolm X's own words reveal a man on the rack. "I live like a man who's already dead," Malcolm X had said a few days earlier. But he retained his courage. "It doesn't

frighten me for myself as long as I felt they would not hurt
my family." Asked about "they," Malcolm X smiled. Then
shaking his head in mock astonishment, he said, "Those
folks down at 116th Street and that man in Chicago." Why
were they after him? "Because I'm me," he replied. "I was
the spokesman for the Black Muslims. I believed in Elijah
Muhammad more strongly than Christians do in Jesus. I
believed in him so strongly that my mind, my body, my
voice functioned one hundred percent for him and the
movement. My belief led others to believe. Now I'm out.
And there's the fear if my image isn't shattered, the Muslims in the movement will leave." Malcolm X was not sure
what he should do at this time. "I won't deny I don't know
where I'm at. . . . But by the same token, how many of us
put the finger down on one point and say I'm here."

In reviewing the Malcolm X autobiography for the *New
Statesman,* Doris Lessing described the curious logic of
Malcolm X's public statements in this period. "Malcolm X
was unable to turn his back on Muhammad," she says near
the end of the review, "but Muhammad had decided to
get rid of Malcolm X. Probably by murder: Malcolm X
thought so—he had himself trained the young men in the
military arts and 'I know what they are capable of,' " Malcolm X had said. Lessing continues: "But he had always
known he would die by violence and 'tried to be ready
for it.' Meanwhile he went to Mecca on pilgrimage, and
learned that what he had been preaching as 'Islam' had
little to do with the real Islam. Race hatred, for instance,
was no part of it." Then Miss Lessing makes her important
point: "This section of [Malcolm X's] book, in which he
is so entertained by Islamic and nationalist leaders in the
Middle East and in Africa, reads embarrassingly like Jenni-
fer's Diary—as painful as the reminiscences of African Nationalist leaders who, taken to the MRA headquarters in

Caux, may return converted because 'they treated me like a human being.' But they seldom stay converted."[33]

Malcolm X did not stay converted. His final speech at Harvard deals with this visit to Africa where he too discovered that he was a human being. Ironically, Malcolm X discovered he was human among brown and black men in Africa.

Malcolm X tried to maintain this humane viewpoint upon his return to the United States. "I believe in the brotherhood of all men," Malcolm X said in his final Harvard speech, "but . . ." he added later, "racists know only one language, and it is doing the black man in this country an injustice to expect him to talk the language of peace to people who don't know peaceful language. Now I say all this in as peaceful a language as I know."[34] It was obviously not a peaceful language at all. It was the rhetoric of the violent hustler and the Black Muslim. Malcolm X complained at one point that (although he wished he could) he was not allowed by circumstances to maintain his new peaceful and humanist position. He blamed others for this failure: "They won't let me turn the corner," he told Alex Haley. They? The explanation did not lie in fixing the blame on someone else; not when the stakes were so high; not when the questions of principle had come clear and he had recognized them; not when he saw a way to leave the "jungle." Instead of a clarity of vision and moral courage, Malcolm X found someone else to blame. His "they" seemed products of his own mind, not a real opposition. Malcolm X's mood in this period of his life is in this phrase from Marx's *Eighteenth Brumaire*: "Men and events appear . . . as shadows that have lost their bodies."[35]

The portrait of Malcolm X that emerges from the quotations above displays the several aspects that made up his life all along, and that befuddled him at the end. Theodore

Jones, who conducted the interview for the *New York Times*, gives us a description of Malcolm X's mood then, his gestures, voice, and manner as he answered questions about himself. Jones saw Malcolm X as an intense person, self-assured, an intellectual of sorts, prone to severe self-analysis. There was first the intellectual and orator; the prison scholar and man of words. "He fingered the horn-rimmed glasses he wore," Jones tells us, "and leaned forward to give emphasis to his words." Malcolm X's gestures were more relaxed at this moment, the pace of his speech slower. He seemed then to retreat very quickly into a private world. "The man, who was once the dynamic spokesman for the Black Muslims," Jones continues, "suddenly leaned forward and began watching the traffic through the large picture window of his private office in the Hotel Theresa. He began talking again, but this time he spoke as if there was only the battered mahogany desk and the rusted three-section filing cabinet in the small room." The very last image Jones gives us of Malcolm X is a mixture of bravado and self-questioning. Jones asked Malcolm X to answer two questions which he thought would expose the contradictions of Malcolm X's recent public statements. "What about the comments by people in Harlem that they do not know where Malcolm X stands? Is it possible to change so suddenly?" Malcolm X was at first confident, pulling at his vest like a successful politician. "He smiled," Jones reports, "opened his black suit jacket, and began rubbing his fingers along the black sweater he wore underneath." The confidence gave way to doubt and then to the now famous assertion of his independence of the Black Muslims. "I feel like a man who has been asleep somewhat and under someone else's control," he said of his Black Muslim career. "I feel what I'm thinking and saying now is for myself. Before, it was and by the guidance of Elijah

Muhammad. Now I think with my own mind, sir."[36] But
Malcolm X's use of the word "sir" showed him still under
Elijah Muhammad's control if only in some unconscious
way. Every Black Muslim used the "sir" in formal address;
it was pronounced sharply and severely. It evoked a sense
of military precision, a commitment by the Black Muslim
members to the prophet and the cult, to the discipline.
Malcolm X was surely still in a state of uncertainty about
the direction and strategy of his branch of the civil rights
movement.

Malcolm X lost the vision of his future in the last few
weeks of his life. He was afraid that he would be assassinated. Instead he was brutally murdered, shot sixteen times,
on February 21, 1965 as he addressed about four hundred partisans at the Audubon Ballroom, Harlem, New
York.

There were four major theories of the assassination: (a)
Elijah Muhammad had Malcolm X murdered; (b) the U.S.
Central Intelligence Agency was responsible; (c) Malcolm
X's disciples and partisans murdered him over an internal
dispute; (d) some self-appointed assassin(s) decided it was
his duty to silence Malcolm X once and for all. Three men
were actually convicted of the deed by jury trial. They were
Thomas Hagan, Thomas Johnson, and Norman Butler.
Despite which theory is correct, Malcolm X's organization
at that time contained a rather curious group of men who
were not all committed to Malcolm X's cause. A bodyguard
of Malcolm X testified at the trial of the convicted men
that he was not sure who in Malcolm X's organization was
friend or foe. "Recalling the confusion at the Audubon
Ballroom . . . Cary Thomas said, 'I decided not to do any
shooting. . . . I was afraid that I might be killed myself.' "
Then referring to the crosscurrents of suspicion that seized
Malcolm X's organization, he added, "I didn't know who

I could tell it to. I didn't know who was who."[37] Indeed
Malcolm X did not know his people. Just before he went
out to speak that day he was surprised by a request
put to him that a young disciple speak ahead of him.
Clearly the effective Black Muslim discipline had not been
imposed on this new group of men. All Malcolm X knew
was that something in his past had caught up with him.
It is very likely that an explanation of the assassination will
be found in the hustler period or among a list of characters
who pursued hustler competition within the Black Muslim
movement. The way Malcolm X was assassinated was brutal
and public, very like a hustler confrontation. A lot of personal hatred lay behind the instructions to the murderers
or in their minds. The assassination was not really very
efficient. Some larger point was being made here, some
lesson was being taught, a sacrifice made, if not before
Malcolm X's followers then before a single man and performed out of a deep and long hatred. Actually a secondary
cause of the assassination can be put forward. The very
extreme principles around which Malcolm X organized
the Black Muslim movement and the Organization of
Afro-American Unity made the thought and justification
of murder all the more easy and the glory of the deed itself
something of value.

What is more, a lesson of history is hidden in Malcolm
X's assassination. It is the lesson of a kind of historical
tragedy. At the beginning of this essay, Malcolm X's life
was linked to the life of his father. The claim was made
that the history of radical Negro movements repeated itself
with these two men. That argument meant to convey that
black nationalist history stood still, constantly repeated its
cycle because of the racist and consequently narrow view
of men held by its partisans. Besides, the political arrangements of black nationalism were very fitful and many sim-

ply products of the imagination. The black nationalist only
rallied to the banner of race. Modern and politically progressive ideas were thought irrelevant, indeed, the weapons
of the white enemy. In the end, black nationalist strategy
was authoritarian and sought out someone to oppress within or without the group; but any oppressed people never
remained docile forever, as the black nationalists proved
by their very existence. Moreover, in the end, other people
found the nationalist, with his white counterpart, the real
obstructionist of progressive and humane government.

The men in these movements, to use the animal imagery
Malcolm X employed so effectively, were very like moles
who were constantly buried by the earth. Jan Kott in discussing just the kind of historical tragedy we see with Malcolm X described the mole's fate. "A mole lacks awareness," Kott said, "but digs in a definite direction. It has
dreams but they only dimly express its feeling for the sun
and sky. It is not the dreams that set the direction of its
march, but the movement of its claws and snout, constantly digging up the earth. A mole will be tragic if it
happens to be buried by the earth before it emerges to the
surface." Malcolm X did not emerge to the surface, or if
he did, it was not for long. A mole was also tragic when it
realized that the earth would go on burying it. The "mole
suffers, feels, and thinks," Kott said, "but its sufferings,
feelings and thoughts cannot alter its mole's fate."[38] Malcolm X knew he was being buried. And when he spoke of
"they" he merely sought to render his ominous circumstance personal, to bring it inside his head and thus try
to understand what was happening to him; to think, perhaps, of some other banner that would rally less desperate
and cruel men to his side. Here, in the end, Malcolm X
disclaimed any victory for himself in his career. He seemed
almost to want to wish away even what he had achieved

for the nation: namely, an increased awareness of the Negroes' anger.

Black people in this country have no peace and have not made the strides forward that would in any way justify receiving a reward by any of us. The war is not won nor has any battle been won.[39]

Well said, old mole! Canst work i' th' earth so fast? A worthy pioneer!

(Hamlet, i, 5)

But if there was tragedy with Malcolm X's assassination it was of no different order than that of his father. Malcolm X had challenged the order of society. He had constantly said change must be made to occur, by any means necessary. He talked sometimes as if he could become an assassin. But if Malcolm X had become an assassin, would it have been for a "noble cause," to free the Negro? Some would surely argue, yes. The irony in this course of action was that the very means of rebellion, the violent deed, could be appropriated by anyone, by white racists in Lansing, Michigan, and by hired Negro assassins in Harlem, New York. Men were equally cruel in murder. The two groups who murdered Malcolm X and his father—one white, the other black—achieved an equality America had denied them. A further equation of equality could be drawn in Malcolm X's assassination. Malcolm X, a "leader" of the Negro people and his obscure Negro assassins were made equal in their violent talk and made doubly equal in the face of death. Shakespeare said just this in *Richard III.* Shakespeare presented there an equation of a hired assassin with the King's brother.

CLARENCE: In God's name, what art thou?
FIRST MURDERER: A man, as you are.

CLARENCE: But not as I am, royal.

FIRST MURDERER: Nor you as we are, loyal.

(*Richard III*, I, 4)

The political creeds of Clarence and the murderers were equally cruel. The banners these sort of men rallied around often held cruel political symbols. Society could not be preserved on either basis. In order for society to survive, each man had to learn to fear his own cruelty, before he was indeed ground down by the very social order he had set in motion by his political creed. Jan Kott discussed the scene from *Richard III* in an essay on Shakespeare's Kings: "Only yesterday Clarence could, on the King's behalf, order [the same assassins] to commit any murder. Today he is in prison himself, and must die by the order, and in the name, of the same King. The Duke [Clarence] and the hired assassins are only men, and cogs in the same mechanism."[40] For Malcolm X, the mechanism was the order of a once perfect world that had been violated, so that evil produces evil, every injury calls for revenge, every crime causes another.[41] Malcolm X's "they" seemed to move about him in those days, shadows, cogs of the mechanism, assassins. As he waited for the assassins, Malcolm X described them. They were partially of his own creation. Finally he was confronted. In the end, "they" were Negroes with blazing guns. Malcolm X had also described elsewhere the violated order of the once perfect world of Elijah Muhammad that now ground him down. Three days before his death, Malcolm X was thoroughly overwhelmed by his circumstances. "I live like a man who's already dead," Malcolm X said. But Malcolm X thought that history would absolve him and his work. "I have dared to dream to myself—which disturbed the white man's smugness, and his arrogance, and his complacency—that my voice helped to save America from a grave, possibly even a fatal catastrophe."[42]

It seemed likely, however, that to stop the mechanism, men had to possess scruples and some measure of doubt about their powers. In *Richard III,* one of the hired assassins experienced a brief moment of doubt.[43]

FIRST MURDERER: What? Art thou afraid?
SECOND MURDERER: Not to kill him, having a warrant; but to be damn'd for killing him, from the which no warrant can defend me.

(*Richard III,* I, 4)

But could one ask the Negro at the bottom to take on the burden of making sound moral judgments? Some would argue that all the weight of injustice which the Negro bore excused him from this requirement. Malcolm X certainly played the role of the judge. To hear him tell it, American society was mostly rotten, fit only for the trash can of history. It was more complicated than that, of course. Malcolm X read history as if it were a personal autobiography. As a result, the clear distinction he made between good and bad was rendered acceptable both by argument and emotion. Malcolm X also behaved as if he held power in his hands, the power of a judge. But once Malcolm X came to the top, once he was a leader, the rules of democracy required that his use of power be called into question; not only the rules of democracy, but also the fear of those below that the new King might demand someone's head some day. In the end, it was perhaps more important to acknowledge the fear one felt in the gut, a fear born of the suspicion that the worst of Malcolm X was merely a mirror-image of American society. And any Negro knew what cruelty stood hidden in that society's history, its office buildings, and back alleys, for us all. Finally a very concrete question had to be considered. Could any practical policy be drawn from Malcolm X's rhetoric?

III. IMAGERY AND IDEAS

An analysis of Malcolm X's language is a way to begin to understand his thought. His conception of society and history were often hidden behind imagery. This is not unusual for Negro orators. In fact, Ralph Ellison sees the use of indirect reference of this sort characteristic of the Negro group as a whole. It is at once a defense against saying what one is really afraid to say because it is rebellious, and at the same time, a kind of secret language for the expression of one's true sentiments. Malcolm X's language reflects most specifically the Negro experience in America. In that sense, to follow Ellison, it had

to do with a special perspective on the national ideals and the national conduct, and with a tragicomic attitude toward the universe. It has to do with special emotions evoked by the details of cities and countrysides, with forms of labor and with forms of pleasure; with sex and with love, with food and with drink, with machines and with animals; with climates and with dwellings; with places of worship and places of entertainment; with garments and dreams and idioms of speech; with manners and customs, with religion and art, with life styles and hoping, and with that special sense of predicament and fate which gives direction and resonance to the Freedom Movement.[44]

Malcolm X was most successful at describing the special sense of predicament and fate of the Negro freedom movement. He had identified what he thought a paradox in Reverend Martin Luther King's non-violent civil rights movement; a paradox, indeed, which was actually at the heart of Black Muslim policy instead. Malcolm X stated it this way: "Anytime a shepherd, a pastor, teaches you and me not to run from the white man, and, at the same time, teaches us not to fight the white man, he's a traitor to you and me."[45] Malcolm X assumed that a victim of racism had either to cringe or attack. He could not support a strategy of passive neutrality; for in accepting neutrality the Negro accepted the status quo. Malcolm X realized later that Elijah Muhammad had served the status quo more than Reverend King. Muhammad had kept the Black Muslims praying in their temples while Martin Luther King actually led the Negro crowds of Birmingham in their protest marches. Malcolm X urged the Black Muslims to transform this paradox into an active, if not violent, strategy. Indeed, when he got his chance, Malcolm X urged the Negroes to adopt a full-fledged violent strategy, nearly anarchist in means. As we shall see, Malcolm X's language was full of descriptions of the violent nature of American society. He believed that the white and black races were at war. He described a cruel and violent conflict. The only way that Negroes could cope with the society was to become beasts of prey. He said of the whites:

> Get the ape off our backs.[46]

> _

> [It] used to be like an eagle, but now it's
> more like a vulture. It used to be strong
> enough to go and suck anybody's blood whether
> they were strong or not. But now it has become
> more cowardly, like the vulture, and it can
> only suck the blood of the helpless.[47]

The whites often hid their true identity from the Negroes, but Malcolm X exposed them.

> You can let those hooded people know
> ....Those were........snakes.

> Those were twenty-one snakes that killed those
> three brothers in Mississippi. . . . There is
> no law in any society on earth that
> would hold it against anyone
> for taking the heads of those snakes.[48]

It was also difficult for the Negro to distinguish the Negro
friend from the Negro enemy in this war. The Negroes
were also animals.

> . . . I hear a lot of you parrot what the [white] man says.[49]

– –

> Our leaders . . . are parrots.
> It's like running from the wolf to the fox.[50]

In Malcolm X's semantic sphere, all through his public
career, there "continually stand out—as word-slogans, word-
clues, evocative words—names of things and animals arous-
ing" evil and fear (Kott). At his father's funeral in 1931,
Malcolm watched in horror "a big black fly come down and
land on [his] father's face."[51] Malcolm, the hustler, talked
of wolves, foxes, ferrets, snakes, vultures; and described a
jungle in which animals (as men) hunted one another. As a
Black Muslim, animals and cosmic bodies invaded Malcolm
X's world, embodying Allah's retribution against the whites
and signaling the impending destruction of American society. When Malcolm X thought himself followed by assassins in 1965, he located himself in a jungle and said, "those
who would hunt a man need to remember that a jungle also
contains those who would hunt the hunters."[52] Indeed,
Malcolm X's conception of society was based on two laws
of the jungle: (1) the conflict between natural enemies and
(2) the survival of the fittest.

Used in speeches, Malcolm X's animal imagery had a
practical effect. Malcolm X told men "how to live by show-
ing . . . rival forms of behavior in another idiom."[53] He
taught by example. He gave speeches about lions, for in-

stance, and achieved a clarity of example; for modes of life are more clearly discernible in an alien element. Malcolm X used animal imagery quite naturally, having been exposed to it, no doubt, in his father's sermons and the speeches of other Negro clergy. Marcus Garvey once described himself as a "flea in the collar of my enemies."[54] The hustler society, to which Malcolm belonged, also used this kind of idiom. Negro blues songs were an especially large repository of this bestiary. The old blues singer, Texas Alexander, sang as a "lion, born in the desert."[55] Of all the imagery we find in Malcolm X's speeches, he used the more violent hustler images most frequently. The hustler conception of society was consistent with his theory of history and his plan of Negro revolution.

By naming things and people, Malcolm X divided the world into the good and the bad. As Kenneth Burke suggests, we "act in the code of names by which [we] simplify or interpret reality. These names shape our relations with our fellows. They prepare us *for* some functions and *against* others, *for* or *against* the persons representing these functions. The names go further: they suggest *how* you shall be for or against. Call a man a villain, and you have the choice of either attacking or cringing."[56] Call a white man a beast, as Malcolm X did, and the same alternatives apply. The white man was a dog, wolf, fox, and a snake.

Even more characteristic was Malcolm X's use of the Biblical images of darkness and light. In his orthodox Black Muslim period, Malcolm X believed that he (and other Black Muslims) lived in a jungle. Malcolm X's jungle contained dark, dangerous places waiting to engulf him, and shafts of light here and there illuminating a way out, allowing him to escape from the beasts that lurked in the shadows. The jungle and society contained two kinds of animals and two kinds of men: the strong and the weak.

At night, the white men (white dogs) were stalked by ghoul-ish, half-human Negro creatures—the black cats (Negro men); by a black, big-headed mad scientist (Yacub), in-ventor of the whites; the wide-eyed incarnation of God (W. D. Fard, Elijah Muhammad's teacher); and, an all-powerful dangerous prophet (Elijah Muhammad) who, through superior mental powers, could cause a man to lose his mind, to lose his way in the jungle. The Negro crea-tures were stalked in turn by the white creatures.

Every Black Muslim believed that Elijah Muhammad could also cause the firmament of the jungle to shake, thunder, and spew forth fire, bringing the rule of the white men to an end. Muhammad alone controlled the movement of darkness and light. A Black Muslim was taught that as long as one did not know the truth, he lived in darkness. But once the truth was recognized and accepted, he lived in light, and whoever would then go against it would be punished along with the white men. White men were evil, black men were good. In order to escape the destructive forces loose in the jungle, white men and black men should separate. Ultimately, the order of the society and of the cosmos depended on the proper separation of the races.

Elijah Muhammad in *Message To The Blackman In America*[57] tells of the consequences a Black Muslim faced in rejecting his command to separate the races or in dis-obeying any of his orders. As in most of Muhammad's speeches, cosmic images are in full use here. Muhammad thought rejection would bring about "a disgraceful year's punishment or chastisement (night and day). You will wish that you were dead," he warned. "When night comes, you will wish it were day, and when day comes, you will wish it night." According to Muhammad, erratic movement of the sun and stars would signal the dawning of the great separa-tion when "Allah, who has power over all things, is bringing the powers of the sun, moon, and stars into display against his enemies. The fire of the sun to scorch and burn men and the vegetation, and dry up the waters. The moon will bring darkness." First, "the moon will eclipse her light to bring darkness upon man." Secondly, all nature would respond. "The magnetic powers of the moon will bring such tidal waves of seas and oceans as man had never witnessed before: the sea and the waves roaring."[58] The elements of nature and even Malcolm X's hustler bestiary were subordinate to Muhammad's cosmic elements. By analogy, all human creatures, including Malcolm X, were subject to Muhammad.

For fifteen years (1948–1963), Malcolm X believed that only Elijah Muhammad knew the way out of this jungle. And when Muhammad expelled him from the Black Muslim movement in November 1963, Malcolm X, the once confident minister, thought that the world had become unhinged, that chaos and darkness had returned, and that the very order of nature was threatened. Malcolm X used Elijah Muhammad's language to describe what he felt then. "I felt as though something in nature had failed, like the sun, or the stars. It was that incredible a phenomenon to me—something too stupendous to conceive."[59]

Muhammad's cosmic imagery also functioned as the political symbolism of the Black Muslim movement. Muhammad's control of cosmic forces implied his control over every Muslim's life and, beyond that, of the destiny of Negro and white Americans. Muhammad was omnipotent and omnipresent. His *symbols of retribution* (sun, moon, water, sky, wind) and *harbingers of madness* (symbolized in the five points of the Muslim insignia, the star, which represented the five senses in Muhammad's brain that sought out hypocrites and infidels) were his agents and served as effective political sanctions against both enemies

and wayward Black Muslims. Fear of this divine retribution was one basis of Black Muslim discipline. What is
more, monopoly of this magic insured Muhammad's control of religious and political functions in the movement.
Any attempt by Muslim believers or ministers, even members of Muhammad's family, at religious or political independence, was undercut by Muhammad's exclusive claims
to divinity. How could anyone act apart from Elijah Muhammad? The offending member was put in serious danger
of having Muhammad invoke the harbingers of madness or
the symbols of retribution.

The actual effectiveness of Muhammad's wizardry can
only be measured indirectly. There are a few cases of mys-
teriously induced mental disturbances of Muslims on record. But the case of Malcolm X's brother, Reginald X, and
that of another Black Muslim reported in the Muslim
paper, *Muhammad Speaks* of January, 1966, suggest that
Black Muslim wizardry was used as sanction in the movement, especially during political crises, and that some Muslims, including Malcolm X, believed in its power. Reginald
Little had challenged Muhammad's right to monopoly of
divine power, and Muhammad responded, Malcolm X believed, by deranging Reginald's five senses. The use of cosmic imagery in Malcolm X's description of Reginald's
chastisement illustrates Malcolm's dependence on Elijah
Muhammad for an explanation of Reginald's illness. Malcolm X describes the Reginald episode very thoroughly in
his autobiography. It is important to recount some of the
detail. "Reginald had been suspended from the Nation of
Islam by Elijah Muhammad. He had not practiced moral
restraint. After he had learned the truth and had accepted
the truth and the Muslim laws, Reginald was still carrying
on improper relations with the then secretary of the New
York Temple. Some other Muslim who learned of it had

made charges against Reginald to Mr. Muhammad in Chicago, and Mr. Muhammad had suspended Reginald."[60] Not long after, Reginald, visiting Malcolm in prison, was openly critical of Muhammad's personal behavior. Unable to convince Malcolm of his accusations, Reginald returned to Detroit.

Now the events seem to take place in the realm of the supernatural. Malcolm X continues: "I heard no more about Reginald until one day, weeks later, Ella [Malcolm's sister] visited me; she told me that Reginald was at her home in Roxbury, sleeping. Ella said she had heard a knock, she had gone to the door, and there was Reginald looking terrible. Ella said she had asked him, 'How did you get here?' And he told her, 'I walked.' "[61] Malcolm X accepted the explanation of Reginald's behavior given to the family by Muhammad some months after this meeting. "I believed he *had* walked," Malcolm tells us. "I believed that Allah's chastisement upon Reginald's mind had taken away Reginald's ability to gauge distance and time. There is a dimension of time with which we are not familiar here in the West. Elijah Muhammad said that under Allah's chastisement, the five senses can be so deranged by those whose mental powers are greater than his that in five minutes his hair can turn snow white. Or he will walk nine hundred miles as he might walk five blocks."[62]

The confrontation between Reginald and Malcolm X indeed took place in a strange realm. Describing it, Malcolm X takes us into his world of beasts and cosmic elements. It was the primordial world of Genesis, an outerworld, "an ocean of blackness,"[63] he tells us. Beasts of prey and powerless animals fought it out here. Reginald was a minnow; Malcolm was a large fish poised, waiting to devour the weaker fish. Malcolm transports us back in time to the beginning of man's creation. In Black Muslim doctrine, the initiate of the movement (here Malcolm) was indeed born anew amidst the upheavals of the cosmos. The visiting room of the Charlestown Prison where the brothers met was transformed into a scene of both cosmic and social conflict.

Malcolm X interprets Reginald's mental illness in a political framework. The law of the jungle prevailed: "The strong shall inherit the earth." We see a terrifying scene through Malcolm's eyes. Reginald thought himself surrounded by snakes, descendants of the serpent who had changed the Garden of Eden into a jungle. Reginald "nervously moved about in his chair; he told me," Malcolm recalls, "that each hair of my head was a snake. Everywhere he saw snakes." But Reginald's clear state of mental illness drew a hustler's reaction from Malcolm. The Bible claimed that "the meek shall inherit the earth." Malcolm X turned this theory on its head: he believed in the survival of the fittest. "I believe," Malcolm X says, "that it was written, it was meant, for Reginald to be used for one purpose only: as a bait, as a minnow to reach into that ocean of blackness where I [was] to save me."[64]

Cruelty and violence were major ideas behind Malcolm X's imagery, even in the hustler period. And much later when he talked of revolution in the Audubon speeches in Harlem (1964–1965), he moved easily between the hustler idiom and the theory of society and history he had received from Elijah Muhammad. Hustler societies used this same kind of violent language to describe conflict among their members. The hustler tradition assumed that human relationships were like those of animals. Indeed, animals imbued with human characteristics informed the hustler's imagination. These animals symbolized (or were like) different groups of men in the hustler society: individualistic men, men who stayed with the herd, courageous men, fearful men, powerful men and weak men. Malcolm X described the traditional and contemporary conflict between the black and white races in the same language. Indeed dialogue between the races can be constructed from Negro hustler blues songs and from Malcolm X's language. The scene is frightful and violent.

White man . . . . Black cat calls me out at midnight.
[My] night mares ride to the break of day. . . .[65]
Negro Man . . . . [The white man] treats me like
a low-down dog.
Hound dog started howlin', somebody's
sure to leave this land. . . .[66]
White Man . . . . You may be as strong as a lion. . . .
You [will] be as humble as a lamb. . . .[67]
Malcolm X . . . . Our leaders . . . are parrots.
It's like running from the wolf to the fox.[68]
Negro blues . . . . Black bodies are . . . fruit for the
singer   crows to pluck.[69]

Here are several characteristic parables which Malcolm X appropriated from the hustler tradition and used in his Black Muslim speeches: ". . . If I go home and my child has blood running down her leg and someone tells me a snake bit her, I'm going out and kill snakes, and when I find a snake I'm not going to look and see if he has blood on his jaws."[70] "If a lion is in a cage, his roar will be different from the roar of a lion who is in the forest. But both the lion in the forest and the lion in the cage are lions. That is what matters. Lions love lions; they hate leopards."[71]

The use of images of nature to describe social conflict was also very characteristic of the hustler society of Malcolm X's day. We find it, for example, in a famous blues song of the same period. Billie Holiday's *Strange Fruit* shows the same "consciousness of nature," as we find in

Malcolm X's imagery, a consciousness in which nature appears to men as a "completely alien, all-powerful and unassailable force, with which men's relations are purely animal and by which they are overawed like beasts. . . ." Paradoxically, *Strange Fruit* conveyed a protest against man's powerlessness, and by implication, a Negro protest against anti-Negro sentiment in America. *Strange Fruit* described a lynching in the South. The nature symbolism—drawn from Southern agrarian idiom—was also characteristic of Negro experience with Southern whites. Miss Holiday's indirect reference to white lynchers in the song provided the blues singer a measure of neutrality before the audience; but the point of reference was clearly understood by her audience. The blues song was real history. It was at once a report of an event and evocative of a tragic mood.

> Southern trees bear a strange fruit,
>> blood on the leaves and blood at the root.
>
> Black body swinging in the Southern breeze,
>> strange fruit hanging from the poplar trees.
>
> Here is a fruit for the crows to pluck,
>> for the rain to gather,
>> for the wind to suck,
>> for the sun to rot,
>> for the tree to drop.
>
> Here is a strange and bitter crop.*[72]

The Negro in this song had accepted his fate without protest. Cosmic forces—the sun, wind, rain—conspired with the lynchers to attack even the dead body. Even the tree rejected him: "Here is a fruit . . . for the tree to *drop*." The total passivity of the victim is vividly portrayed in the

* Copyright Edward B. Marks Music Corporation. Used by permission.

images. Although described as a song of protest, *Strange Fruit* did not urge that the audience do anything about the injustice. Its protest was simply in pointing out that lynching had occurred. But Malcolm X's victim would not have accepted this treatment passively. Malcolm X's nature imagery conveyed a strategy of defense and a strategy of retribution against the white lynchers and the white race as we find in these passages:

One can't unite bananas with scattered leaves.[73]

_ _

If [the white man] waits too long . . . he will be responsible for letting a condition develop in this country which will create a climate that will bring seeds up out of the ground with vegetation on the end of them looking like something these people never dreamed of.[74]

In his speech of November 10, 1963, given before the Detroit Conference of Northern civil rights leaders, Malcolm X implied that Negroes should cease being subservient and become like beasts of prey. Only by adopting this strategy could they become truly free. He told the Negroes, "You came to America on a slave ship, in chains like a horse or cow or a chicken. . . . The white man in America is a wolf and the Negro nothing but a sheep."[75]

Malcolm X believed that men lived by the law of the jungle and the law of history: by conflict and retribution. In his last Harvard speech (December 16, 1964), Malcolm X applied his law of history to the Negro situation. He used an "old saying" to make his point. "I don't think anyone would deny," he began, "that if you send chickens out of your barnyard they always come back home. I was an old farm boy myself, and I got into trouble saying this once [about President Kennedy's assassination], but it didn't stop me from being a farm boy. Other people's chickens

don't come to roost on your doorstep, and yours don't go
to roost on theirs. The chickens that this country is responsible for sending out, whether the country likes it or not,
(and, if you're mature, you look at it 'like it is,' someday),
and someday soon, have got to come back home to roost."[76]
He often added an explanation to this theory of history.
"It is a law of nature,"[77] he once said.

A great deal of passion lay behind all this rhetoric. In
the passage above Malcolm X actually repeated his point
several times, as he often did. John Illo argues that "the
frequent repetitions in Malcolm X's rhetoric . . . are com-
munications of the passion that is not satisfied by single
statement, but that beats through the pulses."[78] Here is
Malcolm X repeating himself again. The image of blood
is shaped over and over again. "As long as the white man
sent you to Korea, you bled. He sent you to Germany, you
bled. He sent you to the South Pacific to fight the Japanese,
you bled. You bleed for white people, but when it comes
to seeing your own church being bombed and little black
girls murdered, you haven't any blood."[79] The listener is
taken into the overwhelming picture of the destruction of
human bodies. Quickly he is taken even further into the
midst of Malcolm X's bestiary. The Negro listener becomes
a trained "dog." It was not that Malcolm X wanted the
Negro to reject the cruelty of this bestiary. He simply
wanted the Negro "to bark and bite" of his own free will.
"You bleed when the white man says bleed; you bite when
the white man says bite; and you bark when the white man
says bark."[80]

Observers generally agreed that Malcolm X's oratory was
very effective on a Negro audience. Indeed Illo viewed
Malcolm X's rhetoric as performing the function of actual
revolution. Illo believes that "rhetoric, like revolution, is
a way of redefining reality."[81] He saw Malcolm X using the

crossing of opposing ideas, "not deceptively, not to con-
found realities, but to explore the calculated fantasies of
the American press, to untangle the crossing of image and
reality."[82] Malcolm X once put it this way:

> . . . you end up hating your friends and loving
> your enemies. . . . The press is so powerful in its
> image-making role, it can make a criminal
> look like he's the victim and make the victim
> look like he's the criminal. . . . If you aren't
> careful, the newspapers will have you hating
> the people who are being oppressed and loving
> the people who are doing the oppressing.[83]

In technique, Malcolm X "wished to demonstrate rather
than suggest, he preferred . . . the analogy to the more condensed and poetic metaphor. . . ."[84] Illo is worth quoting at
length on this point. "Metaphors . . . restricted in number,
often suggested truth, like the analogies, by fusing image
and symbol, as in poetry: Blake's little black thing amid
the snow is sensuously and spiritually black, the snow sensuously and spiritually white. Malcolm [X] used the same
deliberate indetermination of perception in this image by
which he characterized white immigrants in America:

> Everything that came out of Europe, every
> blue-eyed thing is already an American."[85]

"In trying to defend the thesis that the [Black] Muslims
were a force in the Negro movement though numerically
insignificant," Illo continues, "Malcolm [X] compared
them with the Mau Mau, then condensed an implicit
analogy to a metaphor and, with characteristic . . . simplifi-
cation, expanded and explicated the metaphor into analogy."[86] Malcolm X used a halting style of delivery in such
passages, heightening the dramatic impact of his repetitions.

The Mau Mau was also a minority, a microscopic minority, but it was the Mau Mau who not only brought independence to Kenya . . . but it brought it—that wick. The powder keg is always larger than the wick. . . . It's the wick that you touch that sets the powder off.[87]

Malcolm X took the risk of preaching violence to Negroes because he felt the Negroes were a nearly powerless group. His images of the Negro were always dual-images, usually denoting strength and weakness. Malcolm X used the images that marked his outlook as hustler and, toward the end of his life, as the "African in exile" in America: the jungle, the prison, the lost, happy state of pre-slave life in Africa. All these images were bunched together and projected on Africa. One catches a glimpse of his sadness over the Negro state of impotence in his assessment of the effect which the old image of Africa had on American Negroes. Here he was concerned with the Negro's lack of pride and with the Africa he came to think of as his homeland.

When Malcolm X spoke of Africa, he also spoke in very personal terms. He believed that Negroes had been taught that

Africa . . . [was] a jungle, a wild place where people were cannibals, naked and savage in a countryside overrun with dangerous animals. Such an image of the Africans was so hateful to [Negroes] that they refused to identify with Africa. We did not realize that in hating Africa and the Africans we were hating ourselves. You cannot hate the roots of a tree and not hate the tree itself. Negroes certainly cannot at the same time hate Africa and love themselves. We Negroes hated the African features: the African nose, the shape of our lips, the color of our skin, the texture of our hair. We could only end up hating ourselves. Our skin became a trap, a prison; we felt inferior, inadequate, helpless.[88]

A favorable image of Africa was a source of strength for the Negro. Malcolm X reinterpreted the idea of Africa as a jungle. "Africa was a jungle," indeed, but Malcolm X claimed, it was "rich. A jungle is only a place that's heavily vegetated—the soil is so rich and the climate is so good that everything grows, and it doesn't grow in season—it grows all the time."[89]

Illo makes a tremendous claim for Malcolm X's rhetoric. "The achievement of Malcolm X," Illo began, ". . . seems marvelous. Someone had to rise and speak the fearful reality, to throw the light of reason into the hallucinating world of the capitalist and biracial society that thinks itself egalitarian, that thinks itself humanitarian and pacific. But it was unexpected that the speaking should be done with such power and precision by a russet-haired field Negro translated from conventional thief to zealot and at the end nearly to Marxist and humanist."[90] Illo has surely claimed too much. The actual effect of Malcolm X's rhetoric can only be determined by measuring the response Malcolm X achieved. Observers have generally agreed that the response was overwhelming with Negro audiences. The hard question to ask is however, "What was the basis of that almost magical communication between Malcolm X and his Negro audiences?" The basis of that communication cannot be fully discerned as yet, for we have not even begun research on this aspect of Malcolm X's biography. Tentatively, I think that what Illo suggests elsewhere in his essay is in the right direction. Illo's definition of rhetoric is the place to begin. "Rhetoric is . . . poeticized logic, logic revised by the creative and critical imagination recalling original ideas."[91] Illo returned again to the importance of the integrity of the "original idea" in his essay: "In the rhetoric of Malcolm X, as in all genuine rhetoric, figures correspond to the critical imagination restoring the original idea and to the conscience protesting the desecration of the idea. . . . Rhetoric, like revolution," to make Illo's point again, "is 'a way of redefining reality.' "

What "original ideas" did Malcolm X reclaim for the Negro group? Malcolm X's most attractive themes for Negro audiences dealt with racial discrimination in America. In this sphere, Malcolm X dealt mostly with the legacy of slavery. I shall come to a discussion of slavery in the next section. Malcolm X tried also to accurately describe the conditions under which the Negro minority lived in the Northern cities and the rural South. Malcolm X thought that Negroes lived in a state of violence and cruelty. He claimed that the whites were responsible for most of it. It was precisely Malcolm X's description of the violent relationships between the races that gave his rhetoric such appeal for the Negro group. A (perhaps substantial) segment of the Negro group saw their misfortune resulting solely from racial discrimination. For many Malcolm X's violent language expressed the hatred they felt for whites. Malcolm X's bestiary accurately portrayed their view of American society. The races were at war. When a leader of the Black Panther Party of Alabama described the party's strategy, he used language similar to Malcolm X's. The black panther is a "vicious animal, . . ." the leader began. "He never bothers anything, but when you start pushing him, he moves backwards, backwards, backwards into his corner, and then he comes out to destroy everything that's before him."[92]

Malcolm X struck a very resonant chord in the Negro group when he used the language of the Negro folk tradition. As Kenneth Burke suggests, by naming things Malcolm X showed the Negro whom to be against and how to be against him. Malcolm X seemed to express the real feelings of the Negroes about their violent state of existence.

Malcolm X did not invent these ideas. He did not create his bestiary. Indeed, if one is to document the basis of communication between Malcolm X and his Negro audiences, it is to be found in the "fit" of Malcolm X's ideas with an established body of ideas held by the Negro group. The language of recent Negro riots seemed to echo Malcolm X's rhetoric, as if he had loosened the tongues of the Negro lower class.

They think we're savage animals here. . . . They can't tell us what to do, how to live. How can a cat tell a dog what to do?[93]

IV. THE YOKE OF SLAVERY

Malcolm X described the Negro predicament in other terms as well. A major theme of Malcolm X's speeches was the idea that American Negroes lived under the yoke of slavery. As an explanation of Negro history, the idea was not new. In fact it can be found in the speeches of Elijah Muhammad and in speeches of other Negro nationalist prophets before Muhammad. Muhammad told this parable to a public rally at Atlanta, Georgia, in 1961 to illustrate the theory: "The so-called Negroes fell into the hands of the slave-masters, who have robbed, spoiled, wounded and killed them. The Good Samaritan here would be the Mahdi [Allah]—God in person. . . . This one will befriend the poor . . . and heal their wounds by pouring into their heads knowledge of self and others and free them of the yoke of slavery and kill the slave-masters. . . ."[94] Muhammad's theory also contained a solution to the Negro problem. If the Negro accepted Allah as God and Muhammad as prophet, the yoke of slavery could be removed.

The theory of the yoke of slavery, as we find it in Malcolm X's day, took many forms; but in its main outlines it ran as follows: Before 1619 the Negro inhabitants of this country lived as free and happy citizens of African tribes, governing themselves through humane democratic institutions. The slave trade had taken them out of this happy state, tore tribes and families asunder, divested them of their culture and high civilization, and established the tyranny of the white master over the slave. Their women were desecrated and their men emasculated. But the people did not forget the liberty they had enjoyed on the mother continent. Like the Hebrew children, they believed God would deliver them from oppression someday. They had but to pray until the right leader appeared, for the anointed of God to arise and establish the old happy African state in America or lead them across the sea, back to Africa.

Malcolm X accepted the broad outlines of the theory. In addition, he applied the theory to the contemporary Negro situation. In his Atlanta University speech of 1962, he put it in these terms: ". . . From the very same slave-master whom our foreparents had made rich, by giving freely of their slave labor for nearly four hundred years, we received only the hardest and the dirtiest jobs at the lowest wages."[95] Malcolm continued indeed to describe the life of the Negro in the twentieth century. He continued, we have "the poorest houses in the ghettos at the highest rents; the poorest food and clothing at the highest prices. Our schools are like shacks, and were staffed by teachers who knew and could teach only that which the slave-master dictated to them." Following Black Muslim doctrine, Malcolm X argued that Negroes still retained their slave names: ". . . names such as Jones, Smith, Powell, King, Bunche, Diggs, Dawson, etc. These are all slave names, names of the very same slave-master who has shown characteristics of his beast-like nature in his treatment of us. . . . We have really been robbed!"[96] The last four names were actually those of incumbent Negro leaders who, Malcolm was to argue by implication, were equally guilty of keeping the yoke of slavery around the necks of the poor Negro. He believed that every Negro should refuse to take part in the oppression of his own race. Accordingly, any truly free Negro would also refuse to use his slave name, the name given to him by the masters, and take instead the surname every Black Muslim took—X.

The theory of the yoke of slavery was also employed recently in a psychological version in an essay by Johnie Scot, a poet-essayist of the Watts Riot of 1965. Scot saw the effects of slavery expressed in the Watts Riot and, more generally, in the personalities of the radical leaders of the civil rights movement. "The broken family and the image of the emasculated male are a tradition ascribed to the Negro since slavery," he began. "It is a way of life begun by the slavemasters who sold father, mother and son down the river, who callously raped the black man's wife while she, screaming in her agony, lost respect for a man who would not risk death for her. This emasculated male, this man stripped of his manhood, is now at the forefront of the battles for civil rights. It is, for him, the final assertion of his masculinity."[97]

In Malcolm X's hands, Scot's theory of the origin of this leadership was more dialectically conceived and formed the basis of a rudimentary theory of Negro social class set forth (at the earliest) in a speech delivered at the Detroit Conference of Northern Negro Leaders in 1963.

According to that speech, there were two types of Negro leaders at the forefront of the civil rights movement: Uncle Toms or black nationalists; conservatives or radicals. These leaders represented the Negro middle class and the lower class. Malcolm X traced the origin of these classes and the type of leaders back to the days of slavery.

There were two kinds of slaves, the house Negro and the field Negro. The house Negroes—they lived in the house with the master, they dressed pretty good, they ate good. . . . They loved the master more than the master loved himself. . . . If the master's house caught on fire, the house Negro would fight harder to put the blaze out than the master would. If the master got sick, the house Negro would say, "What's the matter, boss, we sick?" And if you came to the house Negro and said, "Let's run away, let's escape, let's separate," the house Negro would look at you and say, "Man, you crazy. What you mean, separate? Where is there a better house than this?"

On that same plantation, there was the field Negro. The field Negroes—those were the masses. The Negro in the field caught hell. He ate leftovers. In the house they ate high on the hog. The field Negro was beaten from morning to night; he lived in a shack, in a hut. . . . He hated his master. He was intelligent. When the house caught on fire, he didn't try to put it out; that field Negro prayed for a wind, for a breeze. When the master got sick, the field Negro prayed that he'd die. If someone came to the field Negro and said, "Let's separate, let's run," he didn't say, "Where are we going?" He'd say, "Any place is better than here!" You've got field Negroes in America today. I'm a field Negro. The masses are the field Negroes. When they see this man's house on fire, you don't hear the little Negroes talking about "our government is in trouble." They say, "The government is in trouble."[98]

How could the Negro masses become free? How could the yoke of slavery be thrown off? Malcolm X believed that first the Negro needed to understand his history in America. Only then could he solve his current problems. He believed that Negro history was primarily the history of some form of Negro slavery extending from the seventeenth century into the present. "You're nothing but ex-slaves," he told the predominantly Negro audience in Detroit. He believed that whites were using essentially the same strategy against the Negro today as was used during slavery. He claimed, "Just as the slave-master of that day used Tom, the house Negro, to keep the field Negroes in check, the same old slave-master today has Negroes who are nothing but modern Uncle Toms, twentieth-century Uncle Toms, to keep you and me in check, to keep us under control, keep us passive and peaceful and nonviolent."[99]

The second step needed was for Negroes to agree on a secular strategy. To begin with, the so-called Negro revolution should be more precisely defined. In defining the revolution, Malcolm X put himself in opposition to Martin Luther King's nonviolent strategy and to the conservative Negroes. "Sometimes I'm inclined to believe that many of our people are using this word 'revolution' loosely. . . . There's no such thing as a nonviolent revolution. Revolution is bloody, revolution is hostile, revolution knows no compromise, revolution overturns and destroys everything that gets in its way. . . . A revolutionary wants land so he can set up his own nation, an independent nation. The [nonviolent] Negroes aren't asking for any nation—they're trying to crawl back on the plantation."[100] The field slaves would only choose the way of a bloody revolution.

From 1963 onwards, Malcolm X became increasingly impatient with the apocalyptic prophecy of Elijah Muhammad. Muhammad kept the Black Muslims praying in the temples while Negro demonstrators, children and adults, braved the dogs and waterhoses of white police in Birmingham, Alabama, and elsewhere in the South. Martin Luther King stirred up the people at the grass-roots level only to teach them to suffer peacefully. Malcolm X saw the nonviolent strategy as produced by the slave mentality. He told the Detroit Conference,

That's Tom making you nonviolent. When [the white man] wants to put knots on your head and take advantage of you and not have to be afraid of your fighting back . . . he gets these old religious Uncle Toms to teach you and me, just like novocaine, to suffer peacefully. Don't stop suffering—just suffer peacefully. As Reverend Cleage pointed out, they say you should let your blood flow in the streets. This is the way it is with the white man in America. He's a wolf—and you're a sheep. Any time a shepherd, a pastor, teaches you and me not to run from the white man and not to fight the white man, he's a traitor to you and me. Don't lay down a life all by itself. No, preserve your life, it's the best thing you've got. And if you've got to give it up, let it be even-steven.[101]

Malcolm X's Detroit speech centered on the Birmingham Riot of 1963. This riot was, for him, the watershed of contemporary Negro history. The black masses had finally thrown off the yoke of slavery, if only temporarily. He even saw the original idea of the March on Washington of 1963 as growing out of the Birmingham Riot. Initially, he argued, the March was to have been an all-Negro event. But Malcolm X claimed that conservative Negro leaders took it over; and it became racially integrated, nonviolent, and ineffective.

The Negroes were out there in the streets [all across the country]. They were talking about how they were going to march on Washington. Right at that time, Birmingham had exploded, and the Negroes in Birmingham—remember, they also exploded. They began to stab the crackers [Southern whites] in the back and bust them up 'side their head. . . . That's when Kennedy sent in the troops down in Birmingham. After that, Kennedy got on the television and said, "This is a moral issue." That's when he said he was going to put out a civil rights bill. And when he mentioned civil rights bill and the Southern crackers started talking about how they were going to boycott or filibuster it, then the Negroes started talking about . . . they were going to march on Washington, march on the senate, march on the White House, march on the

Congress, and tie it up, bring it to a halt, not let the government proceed. They even said they were going out to the airport and lay down on the runway and not let any airplanes land. That was revolution. That was the black revolution.[102]

The Birmingham Riot was Malcolm X's model of a Negro revolution and the beginning of the final phase of the Negro struggle. A new day would be brought in by the "grass roots," the black masses. The masses were Malcolm X's heroes, and the only leadership he thought legitimate was of that group. Malcolm X dated the emergence of this new leadership also at 1963, from the desegregation movements in Albany, Georgia, and Birmingham, Alabama. Both movements had marked the failure of nonviolent strategy. Malcolm X told the Detroit Conference:

When Martin Luther King failed to desegregate Albany, Georgia, the civil rights struggle in America reached its low point. King became bankrupt almost, as a leader. The Southern Christian Leadership Conference was in financial trouble; and it was in trouble, period, with the people when they failed to desegregate Albany, Georgia. Other Negro civil rights leaders of so-called national stature became fallen idols. As they became fallen idols, began to lose their prestige and influence, local Negro leaders began to stir up the masses. In Cambridge, Maryland, Gloria Richardson; in Danville, Virginia, and other parts of the country, local leaders began to stir up our people at the grass-roots level. This was never done by these Negroes of national stature. They control you, but they have incited you or excited you. They control you, they contain you, they have kept you on the plantation.[103]

The final irony for Malcom X was that now the yoke of slavery was held on the neck of the black masses by Negro leaders.

Malcolm X had now reached the high point of his Detroit speech. He was thoroughly secular in language and in ideology, more radical even than the Black Muslims. Specifically, Malcolm X no longer drew the analogy between Hebrew slavery and Negro slavery. God would not deliver the Negro from bondage through heavenly intervention as Elijah Muhammad had promised. The Negro masses had better free themselves. There was indeed no mention of Elijah Muhammad at all in the core of the Detroit speech.

Malcolm X shocked the Detroit Conference by discussing revolution. The anarchists at the Conference were overjoyed to hear him espouse a policy they had advocated all along. Malcolm X had finally taken up their question: "Why wait?" The record made of the Conference has preserved the boisterous reception Malcolm X's strategy evoked. The delegates applauded his call to revolution with tremendous enthusiasm. One can hear the anarchists shouting such a phrase as "We're ready!" But, in practice, Malcolm X remained a Black Muslim minister. Muhammad had fitted him to theorize about revolution, not to make it.

From 1963, Malcolm X's theory of the yoke of slavery became more secular and consequently more attractive to a larger group of Negroes. It was, in fact, Malcolm X's rejection of the religious version of the theory that had rendered him more attractive to the radical leadership at Detroit. The membership of the Detroit Conference were mostly all secular Negro leaders. Among those in attendance at the Conference were "Gloria Richardson (Cambridge, Maryland); Reverend Albert Cleage, Detroit, Michigan, founder of the Michigan Freedom Now Party; Reverend Laurence G. Henry, desegregater of northern Virginia; William Worthy, Baltimore, Maryland, news correspondent and traveler to Red China; Dan Watts, Harlem, New York, publisher of the *Liberator* magazine . . ."[104]

The secular version of the theory dealt mainly with the

strategy by which the Negro masses could win freedom.
Accordingly, the Negro masses faced two equally dangerous
enemies: conservative Negroes and the whites (who were
by nature conservative). Actually a secular version of the
theory had been already put forward by Marcus Garvey in
1921 and hinted at by the Harlem Renaissance poet
Countee Cullen in the epic poem "Black Christ" in
1928.[105] Garvey said that "prayer alone is not going to improve our conditions, nor can the policy of watchful waiting." The Negro "must strike out for . . . [himself] in the
course of material achievement and by our own effort and
energy present to the world those forces by which the progress of man is judged." Garvey then discussed his Negro
opposition referring again to the legacy of slavery.

Our own racial critics criticize us as dreamers and fanatics, and
call us benighted and ignorant, because they lack backbone.
They are unable to see themselves creators of their own needs.
The slave instinct has not yet departed from them. They still
believe that they can only live or exist through the good graces
of their "masters." The good slaves have not yet thrown off
their shackles, thus to them, the U.N.I.A. is an "impossibility."
It is the slave spirit of dependence that causes our so-called
leading men to seek the shelter, leadership, protection and
patronage of "the master" . . . .[106]

Countee Cullen portrayed the effects of slavery on a
southern Negro family of the 1920's in an extraordinary
poem entitled "The Black Christ." Instead of being crucified, the Negro Christ is lynched. The spectators of this
event are an old slave woman and her son. As the poem
unfolds, the lynch-victim is revealed to be the woman's
youngest son. The old woman, nevertheless, clings to her
religion for solace. The older son seeing his brother hang-
ing from the tree exclaims,

God, if He was, kept to His skies,
And left us to our enemies.

Cullen began the poem with the religious version of the
yoke of slavery.

Once there had been somewhere as now
A people harried, low in the dust;
But such had seen their utter trust
In Heaven and its field of stars
That they had broken down their bars,
And walked across a parted sea
Praising His name who set them free.

The secular version of the theory began with the older
son's doubting that God would "set the Negro free."

But in my heart a shadow walked . . . .
. . . There were too many ghosts
Upon its lanes, too many hosts
Of dangling bodies in the wind,
Too many voices, choked and thinned,
Beseeching mercy on its air.

. . . There swung
In all his glory, lusty, young,
My Jonathan, my Patrocles,

And I had neither sword nor song,
Only an acid-bitten tongue,
Fit neither in its poverty
For vengeance nor for threnody,
Only for tears and blasphemy.

Anger smote me and much despair
Seeing her still bow down in prayer.
'Call on Him now,' I mocked . . . while I
With intent equally as sane,
Searching a motive for this pain,

Will hold a little stone on high
And seek of it the reason why.
I mocked her so until I broke
Beneath my passion's heavy yoke.

Cullen criticized the piety of the mother. But the man
who appears at the end of the poem to show the survivors
how to react to the tragedy is "the anointed of God," not
a fierce man of the scum whom Malcolm demanded as a
leader of the former field slaves. And yet Cullen's oldest
son begins to take on the attributes of this leadership, if
only briefly. But Cullen has the oldest son finally confess
his sin of blasphemy. The religious way was the right way
after all.

Let me, the sin-fullest, kneel first;

O Form immaculately born,
Betrayed a thousand times each morn,
As many times each night denied,
Surrendered, tortured, crucified!
Now have we seen beyond degree
That love which has no boundary;
Our eyes have looked on Calvary.

Malcolm X's theory of the yoke of slavery also appeared
in religious and secular versions. Malcolm X was very ambiguous over the whole theory. At first, Malcolm X believed that Elijah Muhammad was the anointed leader
come to lead the American Negro from the land of bondage. Muhammad met one of Malcolm X's criteria of leadership: he was indeed a man of the masses. Muhammad was
not, however, the activist Malcolm X thought this leader
ought to be. For Malcolm, an activist was, in the nature of
the case, less concerned with otherworldly matters. On the
face of it, the Black Muslim movement did evidence a concern for worldly things, but almost exclusively monetary.

Essien-Udum has shown that Muhammad's economic policy seriously sought to satisfy the middle-class aspirations of members of the Black Muslim movement.[107] The Black Muslim system of taxation (used for capital accumulation) and the array of small business enterprises attached to each Muslim temple resulted from this policy. Black Muslim temples were both religious and economic institutions. But what Malcolm X sought finally to add to the Black Muslim ideology was an explicitly political policy which would move the Muslims closer to the intuitive radicalism of the hustler members and of the explicitly radical civil rights groups.

What is more, Malcolm X thought Black Muslim members should have been in the streets of Birmingham with other Negroes during the riot of 1963. He believed the Muslim movement should move toward the kind of people who had swelled its ranks in the decade of the 1950's. Ironically, Malcolm X had obtained permission from Elijah Muhammad to go to Birmingham during the riots, only to be blocked from appearing there by other Negro leaders. Malcolm X was furious. "Asked what he thought of the events at Birmingham, Malcolm X said: 'Martin Luther King is a chump, not a champ!' "[108] The way of nonviolence only led back to the plantation.

The theory of the yoke of slavery was also a theory of a lost happy state of existence. The two goals of Marcus Garvey's UNIA were (1) the liberation of Africa from the colonial powers and (2) the establishment of an independent republic to which Negroes from all over the world could migrate. Garvey's reign over this land would reestablish the old African civilizations. In his final Harvard speech, Malcolm X gave his version of the link between American Negroes and Africa. In Malcolm X's day, African independence had been won; all that was needed was for Negroes to return to Africa, not physically but through acceptance of that part of Africa in every American Negro's soul. Malcolm X put it rather romantically: "We are just as much African today as we were in Africa four hundred years ago, only we are a modern counterpart of it. When you hear a black man playing music, whether it is jazz or Bach, you still hear African music. The soul of Africa is still reflected in the music played by black men. In everything else we do we still are African in color, feeling, everything. And we will always be that whether we like it or not."[109]

Malcolm X would possibly have agreed with Ralph Ellison that the Negroes "thought of themselves as *men* who had been unjustly enslaved. . . ." But Malcolm X would have stressed the need for a political expression of this discontent. His entire message to the Negro group turned on how the Negro should assert his manhood: "How can you thank a man for giving you what's already yours?" The freedom Malcolm X sought for the Negro could not be partial. "How then can you thank him for giving you only part of what's already yours?"[110] Malcolm X called for the kind of personal independence that Africans enjoyed. He urged the Negro to return to Africa.

The African States have emerged and achieved independence. Negro people in this country are crying out for their independence and show a desire to make a fighting stand for it. The attitude of the Afro-American cannot be disconnected from the attitude of the African; the pulse beat, the voice, the very life-drive . . . is reflected [in both]. . . . It is the same heart and the same mind, although separated by four hundred years and by the Atlantic Ocean.[111]

Malcolm X seemed to dress himself in the tattered costume of a slave when he addressed any audience. While standing in the twentieth century he did not look ahead but turned his neck to look back toward the past. The theory of the yoke of slavery actually located him in another era. Malcolm X believed that the hold of a feudal slave era over the mentality of Negro and white had not been broken. The ideology of slavery permeated nearly every policy the whites followed. They behaved like the slave holders of the Old South. Some were kind, and others cruel, but every single white was a slave holder of some sort. The white liberals were a mirror-image of the worst kind. The Negroes, Malcolm X argued, were simply in captivity; nothing they did could change their status. A slave was a slave. If a slave thought himself free, it was because he was living under a delusion. A pretentious free Negro was only a mirror-image of the lowest slave. We saw earlier how Malcolm X's notion of stratification in Negro communities rested on this very reading of history.

Malcolm X compressed history into a single time frame. Negro history was cyclical, always returning to the same starting point. The actors of Negro history in this era merely replayed the old parts of the old drama. They were cut from the same cloth. The scenario always took place on the plantation. What is more, Malcolm X never admitted that the Negro now lived in a different world and that the relationships between the races were qualitatively different. Malcolm X always held up a mirror to contemporary history. And the present and the past were both judged with the same eye. Malcolm X felt, moreover, that the era of slavery had been so cruel that no one should consent to forget it.

Despite these arguments, the idea of a yoke of slavery was archaic in a strict sense. But Malcolm X had something else in mind when he used it. He wanted to deflate a white liberal society and its handmaidens: the complacent Negroes. The complacent holders of power and the wealthy horde had to be deposed from the throne.

Shakespeare described an identical episode in *Richard II*.

Shakespeare also had in mind the comparison of two eras as well as the dethronement of power. *"Richard II* is a tragedy of knowledge gained through experience," Jan Kott tells us. "Just before being hurled into the abyss, the deposed King reaches the greatness of Lear. For King Lear, like Hamlet, is also a tragedy of man contemporary with Shakespeare; a political tragedy of Renaissance humanism. A tragedy of the world stripped of illusions."[112] "Richard II," Kott resumes, "is brutally and suddenly pushed into the abyss. But with him will founder the structure of the feudal world."[113] The feudal world and the Renaissance world will have something in common, nevertheless. Personal and political cruelty will reappear in *Richard III.* Malcolm X argued that the era of slavery and the modern era of segregation had the very same thing in common for the Negro. Richard II also held up a mirror to history and to himself. Richard II saw a face which had once borne a glory compared to the sun. Richard II seemed anxious about his "brittle face," his brittle career.

> Give me the glass, and therein will I read.
> —
> . . . .Was this the face
> That like the sun did make beholders wink?
> Was this the face that fac'd so many follies
> And was at last outfac'd by Bolingbroke?
> A brittle glory shineth in this face.
> As brittle as the glory is the face,
>   (*Dashes the glass to the floor.*)
> For there it is, crack'd in a hundred shivers.
> Mark, silent King, the moral of this sport—
>   (*Richard II,* IV, 1)

Slavery was the single feudal element in American history. The Negro, accordingly, was kept in a rigid status and denied the most fundamental freedoms. Malcolm X read

Negro history as a history of oppression. The sun had set when the slaves had left the shores of Africa. The sun would not rise until the yoke was thrown off. Malcolm X's landscape of Negro captivity showed a very black, terrifying night. His portrait of the slaves showed them in a place of utter desolation. What Malcolm X actually conveyed about the Negro was that the setting of his existence was betwixt the past and the present. He really held to Elijah Muhammad's view that the Negro was of a lost-found tribe. The dual metaphor actually conveyed a profound view of the matter. It had occurred to Elijah Muhammad and Malcolm X that the Negro was in a state of exile in America. "You're nothing but an ex-slave,"[114] Malcolm X would say. But Malcolm X only drew the most awful consequences from being in the state of exile. He only barely understood the tremendous and healthy liberation from the mundane which such a people often achieved. Such a status gave them potentially a more critical and profound vantage-point in the society.

Countee Cullen ended his poem with the Negro mother and son literally back in Africa, having regained their lost rights, their origin and a full life. The son tells us,

> The days are mellow for us now;
> We reap full fields; the heavy bough
> Bends to us in another land;
> The ripe fruit falls into our hand.

Such was the theory. As an historical account of American Negro slavery and subsequent Negro history, it leaves much to be desired. At best it did represent the experience one generation of Negroes passed on to another. Ralph Ellison sees the legacy of slavery as playing an important role for the Negro, nonetheless, if only in memory. "We Negroes have long memories," he claims. "We know what

went on before 1865 and after 1876 [during slavery and
after Reconstruction had been killed]. . . . And if you think
about it, there is hardly a Negro of my generation who
can't touch a grandparent or two and be right back in
slavery—it has been that recent. So, we have within our
very lives and our memories a sense of the reality of slavery
and what has been promised by Emancipation."[115]

Ellison also knows that to speak of slaves and masters in
a modern society is too simple, a fundamentally archaic
formulation and one likely to divert attention from the real
obstruction Negroes faced in the contemporary situation.
The relationship of the American Negro to American society is a complex affair involving the strong influences of
urban existence; the competition among Negroes for
wealth and status; the exploitation of the ghetto Negro by
some whites and (on the other hand) assistance from other
whites; and, as Ellison argues in *Shadow And Act,* the creative use of freedom and imagination by some Negroes to
break out of the bonds of caste and race, leaving their mark
on the society, and changing it in some way. Ellison, in
reviewing LeRoi Jones' *Blues People,* explains that ". . . political categories are apt to confuse, for while Negro slaves
were socially, politically and economically separate (but
only in a special sense even here), they were, in a cultural
sense, much closer than Jones' theory [of slavery] allows
him to admit. 'A slave,' writes Jones, 'cannot be a man.' "
". . . Isn't it closer to the truth," Ellison asks, "that far from
considering themselves only in terms of that abstraction,
'a slave,' the enslaved really thought of themselves as *men*
who had been unjustly enslaved? . . . Slavery was a most
vicious system and those who endured and survived it a
tough people, but it was *not* (and this is important for
Negroes to remember for the sake of their own sense of
who and what their grandparents were) a state of absolute

repression . . . The art—the blues, the spirituals, the jazz, the dance—was what we had in place of freedom."[116]

Malcolm X believed that without Africa the Negro did not even have a culture, he had no roots. By stressing the importance of Africa as a "place of origin," Malcolm X hoped to resurrect what he called a dead people. The existence of a history was essential to any captive people. "Just as a tree without roots is dead," he said, "a people without history or cultural roots also became a dead people."[117] Malcolm X's landscape of Negro captivity was full of gnarled, dead trees, stumps and skeletons. He described it in a vivid, modern language with words painting a mood of the grotesque, full of weeping and wailing. He evoked the groans of slaves packed in the slave ship bottoms centuries ago. Human misery filled the air. The trees and the bones were such symbols of Negro captivity.

> . . . Once our names were taken and our language
> was taken and our identity was destroyed and
> our roots were cut off with no history, we became like
> a stump, something dead. . . . Anybody
> could step on us, trample upon us or burn us.
> - - - - - - -
> When the old preacher started singing about dry bones,
> you'd knock over benches [in Church], just because
> he was singing about those bones . . . .
> . . . But you never could identify the symbolic
> meaning of those bones—how they were dead
> because they had been cut off from their own kind.
> . . . But you shed more tears over those dry bones
> than you shed over your self. This is a strange thing,
> but it shows what happens to a people when they are
> cut off and stripped of everything.
> - - - - - - -
> We have been in a land where we are not citizens,
> . . . in a land where they have treated us as strangers.[118]

V. THE THEME OF EXILE IN
THE HARVARD SPEECHES

Malcolm X saw himself and the Negro group as exiles in a sense akin to that of the stranger and the criminal fugitive. The very society was a jungle for him. He was lost there. Not only lost, but threatened by a daily violence. Even as he became less sectarian in religious views, his assessment of the Negroes' future in the secular sphere remained narrow and reactionary. But Malcolm X's racism, which was considerable, was pieced together helter-skelter, very much the product of his public anger. As a solution, he urged Negroes to seek a new world. This world was actually located in several places during the course of his career. The Harvard speeches reflect these changes in his thought very nicely. The speeches had one thing in common. The locale of his exile was, by imagination and fact, the ghetto of Negro America.

Malcolm X behaved very much like a prophet in the Harvard Speeches. His new world was described in apocalyptic language, which was, for him, the appropriate place to call a halt to the cruel mechanism of American society which held Negro history in its grasp. But each Harvard speech found Malcolm X describing a fantastic and unreal homeland for the Negro. It was first the orthodox Muslim world, then a devastated America, and finally Africa.

Malcolm X continued to call for revolution throughout his public career. But he also urged escape. Revolution was his public strategy. Escape was his private strategy. Malcolm X actually sought this latter strategy only for himself. In speaking before Negro audiences, he sometimes gave his

private strategy away, however. That he did so while advocating revolution was a major paradox of his life and
thought. Malcolm X's new world was, therefore, a very
private hideaway. When he described it to others, with
political strategy in mind, it was inevitably romantic in
character, very like his notion of life in Africa before the
Negro was forced under the yoke of slavery and brought to
America.

The Harvard speeches contain both Malcolm X's public
and private strategies. It is not easy to separate one from
the other, especially since his notion of revolution was
romantic and thus highly personal. Surely Malcolm X
would have discovered that to make revolution in a modern
society requires a thorough comprehension of that society;
requires a revolutionary as modern as is the opponent. Of
course, Malcolm X, like the black power advocates, did not
mean revolution when he used the word. Malcolm X actually called for a "street rumble" of sorts; that is surely different from either revolution or guerilla warfare. What
Malcolm X urged was anomic behavior on the part of the
Negro masses. In this regard, the paradox drawn earlier between his public strategy of revolution and his private strategy of escape very nearly disappeared. Upon closer analysis,
history will show that a strategy of escape really informs
mass outbursts such as the Negro riots of recent summers.
Malcolm X actually betrayed his confusion over the actual
worth of this strategy in the Harvard speeches.

The first Harvard speech was the most romantic. Here
the prophetic style was very pronounced. Since this first
speech occurred at the height of Malcolm X's orthodox
Black Muslim period, the new world was thoroughly apocalyptic in nature. The call to violence in this context was,
curiously enough, merely a side product of a strategy of
escape. The call to violence really served a ridiculous logic:

If the whites won't give us a separate black state in the United States (Malcolm argued), we will wreak havoc on the nation. Why didn't the Black Muslims simply leave? The counter argument was that American whites had to provide the separate state here as some kind of compensation for the free labor exacted from the Negroes over the years. But the Black Muslims and Malcolm X did not really press the point. An alternate solution, equally acceptable to them, was a mass Negro exodus to the orthodox Muslim world.

The theme of exile lay just at the surface of nearly all Malcolm X's formulations in this first Harvard speech. The Black Muslims did not really wish to engage white Americans in battle. The overriding argument of the first Harvard speech was first the destruction of America by apocalyptic means. The new world Malcolm X foresaw would be built atop the rubble of a devastated society. "I must remind you," Malcolm X said, ending the first Harvard speech, "that your own Christian Bible states that God's coming will bring about a great separation." "Then everyone," he concluded, "will be able to live . . . 'under his own vine and fig tree.' " "Otherwise," Malcolm X warned, ". . . all of you who are sitting here, your government, and your entire race will be destroyed and removed from this earth."[119]

The vantage point of the Black Muslims was indeed curious. But there was something of fancy and fact in their preoccupations.

The view of society that informed Malcolm X's first Harvard speech was almost idyllic. His brand of prophecy also hid a barely visible element of the absurd. Was Malcolm X a prophet or a jester? Did he really believe that a small but motley band of men and women, the Black Muslims, represented such ultimate power?

Both the prophet and the jester were exiles living within a society. Each kept himself on an island in fact or in imagination. While the prophet was a religious leader, the jester played his role before the holders of power, before the throne. A jester's audience was a mirror image of his worst self. And his job was to change the frown of the crowd into a smile. There were, of course, sweet clowns and bitter clowns. Malcolm X was a bit of both, full of illusions and sometimes free of them. The bitter clown Thersites in *Troilus and Cressida* "regards the world as a grim grotesque place":[120]

. . . The parrot will not do more for an almond than he for a commodious drab. Lechery, lechery! still wars and lechery! Nothing else holds fashion. A burning devil take them!

(V,2)

The prophet and the jester both performed the role of judge. Jan Kott helps give perspective to the jester's philosophy: "When established values have been overthrown, and there is no appeal to God, Nature, or History, from the tortures inflicted by the cruel world, the clown becomes the central figure in the theatre. He accompanies the exiled trio—the king, the nobleman, and his son—on their cruel wanderings through the cold endless night which has fallen on the world; through the 'cold night' which, as in Shakespeare's *King Lear,* 'will turn us all to fools and madmen.'"[121] The jester was the realist and the pessimist. The prophet was the optimist of the two. Although the prophet forecast destruction, as Malcolm X did, he also held out a glimmer of hope. At the end of the first Harvard speech, Malcolm X admitted there was still hope for America. "Why don't you repent while there is yet time?" he asked.[122] Malcolm X as prophet seemed to peer into an abyss. As jester he often played the role of a madman. In

some speeches, Malcolm X seemed to imagine a white man
in the shape of Gloucester of *King Lear.* "After his eyes
have been gouged out," Kott says of Lear, "Gloucester
wants to throw himself over the cliffs of Dover into the sea.
He is led by his own son [by Edgar] who feigns madness.
Both have reached the depths of human suffering. . . . They
walk together."[123] The scene here could be transferred to
our time. This scene set in America would require a change
in language. Malcolm X, as Edgar, would tell Gloucester
of Negro men below on city streets who look like ants,
dwarfed by a massive modern technology. Gloucester,
played by an American white, would have an answer for
Malcolm X, a comment on the little Negroes below. It is
not Shakespeare's Gloucester who gives us the response relevant to our time, however. Kott found the most meaningful response for us in Slowacki's *Kordian.* This Edgar commanded Gloucester to look into an abyss filled with animals
and men:

> Come! Here, on the top stand still. Your head will whirl,
> When you cast your eyes on the abyss below your feet.
> Crows flying there halfway no bigger are than beetles.
> And there, too, someone is toiling, gathering weed.
> He looks no bigger than a human head.
> And there on the beach the fishmen seem like ants . . .[124]

Malcolm X also saw animals and men living together in
America. It was his way of describing a cruel society. He
was not alone in this view. Recently, two white public officials of American cities saw a similar world below. In their
view, Negroes were the animals. And animals could only
be frightened into flight by fire. If not frightened, they
would certainly be destroyed in the flames of Hell. Bugs
and beetles were plotting to destroy the cities by riot.
Gloucester must listen to these white men. He would then
hear an explanation of what lay below him in our time and

place. To Gloucester's question, 'What lay below?' they would answer:

The degenerate thugs who hide in darkened windows and shoot down police and firemen. . . .[125]

- - - - - - -

One had a solution:

We must fight fire with fire. Fear and only fear will stay those hoodlums from injuring decent people. They must know that when they go to war with the City of Philadelphia they will be fighting a terrible enemy.[126]

Gloucester committed suicide in Kott's *King Lear.* "The blind Gloucester falls over on [an] empty stage. . . . In an Elizabethan production, the blind Gloucester would have climbed a non-existent height and fallen over on flat boards,"[127] being a clown. Gloucester as a jester is difficult to understand except in the theatre and world of Beckett. In that world, animals and men are on the stage together. Beckett's world is our world. It was Malcolm X's world.

[A man] goes and sits down on a big cube. The big cube is pulled from under him. He falls. The big cube is pulled up and disappears in flies. He remains lying on his side, his face towards auditorium, staring before him.

(Beckett, *Act Without Words,* p. 60) [128]

Malcolm X as the clown would not stare ahead. He would smile, and the prophet would appear to become the Uncle Tom. Malcolm X often gave speeches with laughter in his voice. The first Harvard speech was full of this. He predicted destruction, but then he took his words back. "This evening since we are all here . . . together," Malcolm X said, saying it again as if to mock integration, "both races face to face, we can question and examine ourselves the wisdom or folly of what Mr. Muhammad is teaching."[129] Malcolm X would have laughed here, the laughter evoking a hundred years of cynicism among Negroes over white goodwill. He really wished to say something else. "This evening since we are all here together," he would have begun again, "both races face to face, 'fear and only fear will stay these [white] hoodlums.' The evil features of this wicked old world," he would rush to say, as he did say elsewhere in that speech, "must be exposed, faced up to, and removed in order to make way for the new world."[130] Malcolm X, the clown, had become the judge and executioner. He became like a little boy chasing flies.

The image of flies in *King Lear* was taken over from *Othello*. In *Lear* the image of little boys chasing flies, according to Kott, "contains one of man's ultimate experiences":[131]

As flies to wanton boys are we to th' gods.
They kill us for their sport.

(Lear, IV, 1)

DESDEMONA: I hope my noble lord esteems me honest.
OTHELLO: O, ay! as summer flies are in the shambles,
That quicken even with blowing. . . .

(Othello, IV, 2)

Malcolm X assumed that every Negro would very rightly think himself a fly in the hands of white men, of the whites as judge. Malcolm X reversed these roles, of course. Elijah Muhammad was the judge, Malcolm X, the clown before Muhammad's seat of power. The whites were then as flies to a new black god. Left in the hands of the judge, the whites would perish.

White man . . .
'You're a beast; you've got one-third animal blood.'
He is the devil.

(Sermon by a Minister of the
Black Muslim Chicago Temple) [132]

In the face of this assessment of the whites in America, Elijah Muhammad and Malcolm X could only choose two alternatives. They could fight for survival among the whites or leave the society altogether. Elijah Muhammad urged escape, and Malcolm X, repeating after him, in the early period, also urged escape. Elijah Muhammad thought the cities were already filled with fire.

... You don't know yourself nor your enemies; or rather are lost in love for our enemies. I know you, who love your enemy don't like that I tell you this truth. But, I can't help it—come what may. God has put upon me this mission, and I must do His will or burn.

(Elijah Muhammad, *Message To The Black Man*, p. 122)

The rioters of Watts, California, put Elijah Muhammad's admonition into "street language." The rioters, however, did not wish to leave destruction of the society in "the hands of the judge or of God." It was their self-appointed mission to set fire to the society. The very slogan of the Watts riot to burn the city became the password in Negro ghettos across the country. The slogan echoed Elijah Muhammad's imagery of fire. The Watts rioters meant to encourage each other with the call to riot. A bitter clown would have told them the slogan was ironic and indeed suggested self-immolation. The slogan called fire down on the rioters themselves and on the society. They shouted:

Burn, baby, burn!

Malcolm X tried to play the bitter clown during his second Harvard speech. The second speech was hesitant in a new way because he took on this different role. The date of the second speech was, of course, one reason Malcolm X was rather unsure of himself. Two weeks before, he had resigned from (indeed been forced out of) the Black Muslim movement. The dispute with Elijah Muhammad had been over Malcolm X's public indiscretion, his referring to President Kennedy's assassination as "chickens coming home to roost." The dispute had other overtones as well. One such element was the different way Elijah Muhammad and Malcolm X understood the role of leader and defined policy. Malcolm X viewed the chances of achieving the Black Muslim policy of racial separation as impractical for the moment. His private view of the matter seemed sarcastic and ambiguous. It was the view of an embittered leader. The sarcasm was directed at everyone around him; at his lieutenants; at the whites, of course; at the society; and very much at the incumbent Negro leaders. Elijah Muhammad came within this purview, if only by inference. Malcolm X saw himself at the bottom of the heap now, beside the poor Negro folk. He seemed to challenge white and Negro leaders who stood on the top. There was white exploitation and Negro exploitation:

The black people in this country are beginning to realize that what sounds reasonable to those who exploit us doesn't sound reasonable to us. There just has to be a new system of reason and logic devised by us who are at the bottom, if we want to get some results in this struggle that is called the Negro revolution.

(Second Harvard Speech)

What did Malcolm X have in mind? "The only real solution to our problem," Malcolm X began, "just as the Honorable Elijah Muhammad has taught us, is to go back to our homeland and to live among our own people. . . . I still believe [in] this. But that is a long-range program. And while our people are getting set to go back home, we have to live here in the meantime. So in the Honorable Elijah Muhammad's long-range program, there's also a short-range program: the political philosophy which teaches us that the black man should control the politics of his own community."[133]

Malcolm X's short-range program was explicitly sep-aratist in nature. Put simply, Malcolm X urged Negroes to gain control of their communities, reassert African cul-ture and, in the process, prepare to use violence against the whites. Actually, the control of Negro communities, politi-cally and economically, required a prior independence of the larger society and the presence in the community of the "stuff" of modern life. In actuality, the Negro com-munities were not off in Africa somewhere, as Malcolm X often imagined, but were, rather, small impotent parts of a vast modern-industrial complex. The African culture Malcolm X had in mind was not authentic in any way. If Negroes were to reassert the African soul, as he urged, it first had to be conceived and created, and then, probably, only out of the imagination. The utter romanticism of these policies was only outdone by the talk of violence. The call to violence, as was to be seen among the black power partisans, was really a call to madness, confusion, and more separatist policies. Malcolm X did not foresee the cost in Negro life and property these policies would require.

Malcolm X foresaw what it would cost him, however. The second Harvard speech contained a very curious set of disclaimers. The disclaimers marked the limits of Malcolm X's conception of what Negro leadership could accom-plish. "I am not a politician," he said. "I'm not even a student of politics. I'm not a Democrat. I'm not a Repub-lican. I don't even consider myself an American."[134] What was he then? Malcolm X, the Negro and the man, was all that remained of his previous career as a Black Muslim minister. His lowly status was akin to the status of a fugi-

tive. Such a status cost Malcolm X his previous certainty
about his public strategy. He seemed betwixt and between
a new *rite de passage*. The direction of his movement, in
thought at least, was toward a kind of primitive Marxism.
The Negro masses were his true companions. The Negro
masses had been betrayed by incumbent Negro leaders.
Malcolm X had been betrayed by Elijah Muhammad. His
public strategy finally began to convey something of his
realism and pessimism over Negro life chances in contemporary America.

The substance of the public strategy in the second speech
was, however, very pessimistic. Malcolm X's pessimism was
revealed in the pivotal images of exile used at the beginning and at the end of this speech. ". . . The black people,"
he said, "were . . . disenchanted, disillusioned."[135] The
Negro did not wish to integrate with whites; in fact, he
never thought of it. The thoughts most central to the contemporary Negro, according to Malcolm X, had to do with
going back to Africa. Accordingly, Malcolm X always combined images of captivity with images of escape. The Negro
wished to leave the "alley," "ghetto," "penitentiary,"
"bounds," "captivity." The images of captivity were dark
in tonal color. They suggested a sinking motion. Malcolm
X saw the Negro trapped, trapped in "dirt." The Negro
had been "let down." His portrait of the Negro face in
exile was strongly drawn, full of suffering and foreboding.
Malcolm X argued that if his policy was followed, the face
of the Negro exile would stop its bitter wailing. A sad and
dark sky surrounded the landscape of Malcolm X's Negro
captivity. The sun had set. This was not the promised land.
Indeed time and again the white politicians had promised
more. "This feeds the hopes of the people," Malcolm X
said, ". . . and after the politicians have gotten what they
are looking for, they turn their back on the people of our

community." "The black people today," Malcolm X admitted, "are beginning to realize that it is a nightmare to us. What is a dream to you is a nightmare to us. What is hope to you has long since become hopeless to our people . . . in the ghetto, in the alley where the masses of our people live. . . ."[136] The pivotal image of "going home" represented Malcolm X's solution to Negro captivity. It was a very intimate and personal image. The rhetoric associated with it, in one instance, was first of the Negro slang idiom and then romantic in a nineteenth-century manner. "Our people are getting set to go back home . . ."[137] Malcolm X said in one place. And then he combined the image of the family tree with a romantic view of the past and the present. "We will reach back and link ourselves to those roots, and this will make the feeling of dignity come into us; we will feel that as we lived in times gone by, we can in like manner today. If we had civilizations, culture, societies, and nations hundreds of years ago, before you came and kidnapped us and brought us here; so we can have the same today."[138] It is, is it not, a rather heroic view of the Negro past and a rather irrelevant remedy for the present and a mere dream for the future. Separate civilizations and societies were really only possible in the medieval world. Even in slavery, the relationship of the Negro to the larger American society, and thus to modernity, was more intimate than we have been willing to admit. And even if it was not intimate, modernity remains that requirement which the Negro group must meet if it is to cope in the modern world.

Martin Kilson, in an unpublished essay, has said very plainly what shape the pursuit of political modernity must take on if it is to succeed. Kilson had the black power advocates in mind here, but his prescriptions also serve as a critique of Malcolm X's policies. He argued, in one sense, that the leadership group which was capable of performing the task of modernization in Negro communities was, for want of a better term, the Negro tertiary elite. "As a problem," Kilson begins, "the phenomenon of Black Power is one of leadership: where, in what numbers, of what quality and skill, is leadership to be located, capable of meeting the black masses in the ghettoes at their own threshold of existence."[139] He continues: "Even a lower class as structurally incoherent as the Negro lower class has a stratum near it that performs basic leadership roles. We know very little about this group—compared, say, to what is known about the Negro middle and professional classes. . . . It includes such people as owners of flop houses, poolrooms, shoeshine stands, bars, dingy barber shops, grocery and eating places, and numbers writers and other quasi-underworld sorts. This leadership group is awfully small," Kilson concludes, "and, given the limited resources at hand, very restricted in the range of functions it can perform. Yet it is, in some sense, a viable group: it has patterned and predictable arrangements and especially a set of institutionalized interests that must be nurtured and advanced."[140] Most importantly, the tertiary elite has the "attitudes and outlook" basic to such a leadership role.

Malcolm X was of the tertiary elite, as was his father. He had tremendous organizing skills. The Black Muslim movement grew from a mere 400 under Elijah Muhammad to 40,000 under Malcolm X's initiative. But Malcolm X (for personal and ideological reasons) misread the modern world. His long dependence on the religious ideologies of the Black Muslim movement, and later on black nationalism, as sources of a coherent view of the world, left him ill-suited to lead a movement for the political modernization of the Negro group. At the same time, the perpetual sense of crisis and doom that pervaded the final months of his life certainly took a great toll of his energy and intellect.

If Malcolm X misread the modern world on questions of policy and political strategy, he certainly read its philosophy correctly. The chief characteristic of modern life was that "action develops under great stress."[141] Negro life has always developed in a crucible. The third, and final, Harvard speech was an intensely personal speech. Although it alternated between romanticism and realism, it conveyed an intense search by Malcolm X for a humane view toward whites. But Malcolm X played the sweet clown one moment and the bitter clown the very next.

A dispute was going on in Malcolm X's mind about "the existence of a moral order in a cruel and irrational world." The dispute went on in Shakespeare's *Troilus and Cressida*. As Kott suggested, "Hamlet, the Prince of Denmark, [had] faced the same trial."[142] Ironically, Malcolm X used the example of Hamlet in the third speech to symbolize the dispute within him and to justify his call for violence. For Malcolm X, Hamlet was a simple, violent fellow. Hamlet had a right to murder because he had been wronged. "There was another man back in history," Malcolm X began, obviously comparing himself, "whom I read about once, an old friend of mine whose name was Hamlet, who confronted, in a sense, the same thing our people are confronting in America."[143] Hamlet was debating whether he could be himself, Malcolm X argued. Locating himself in the medieval world, Malcolm X claimed that an obvious strategy lay before the Negro and before him. "As long as you sit around suffering the slings and arrows and are afraid to use some slings and arrows yourself, you'll continue to suffer."[144] Malcolm X's Hamlet was also Shakespeare's Prince, a man of high birth, someone betwixt and between things; a dramatic character who was the stuff of heroics and tragedy. Ossie Davis, in Malcolm X's eulogy, called Malcolm X the Negro people's Black Prince. So the world of Malcolm X and the world of Hamlet were similar to Davis at least. But, as Kott suggests, Hamlet can be interpreted in a number of ways. At first, we must not be bothered by the juxtaposition of the medieval and modern world by Ossie Davis—or by Malcolm X for that matter. It does not matter. It did not matter for Malcolm X. What matters was that a Negro man was trapped in exile in the ghetto. Hamlet said Denmark was a prison. He was in exile in his own country, in his own castle. Malcolm X said America was a prison. He was in exile in his own country, and was suffering because of it. What a fate for Malcolm X. He had nearly found his way through the jungle only to find himself trapped again. Besides, he was alone for the first time in his public career. When Malcolm X came to the second Harvard speech he was surrounded by six Negro guards. When he came to the third and final Harvard speech he came alone.

Malcolm X's Hamlet was a moralist and an intellectual and a philosopher, as he was. "The moralist," Kott contended, was "unable to draw a clear-cut line between good and evil. . . . The intellectual [was] unable to find sufficient reason for action: [and to] the philosopher, the world's existence was a matter of doubt. 'To be' means for [Hamlet] to revenge his father and to assassinate the King; while 'not to be' means—to give up the fight."[145] The Negro hustler was distinguished by his capacity to act; to steal or to murder. The Black Muslim minister was distinguished by his ability to find a sufficient reason for action, for giving the Negro folk an ethic, whether it was of hate or of pride. Malcolm X, the man, in the end was not distinguished by anything at all, except, perhaps, by "finding himself in a compulsory situation, a situation he [did] not want but which [had] been thrust upon him. He [was] looking for inner freedom, and did not want to commit himself."[146] But Malcolm X continued his round of speaking engagements after the third Harvard speech. He accepted the choice imposed on him, "but only in the sphere of action."[147] Kott sums up the last few days of Malcolm X's life: He was committed in what he did, not in what he thought. Malcolm X was inwardly starved. "We should take political action," Malcolm X said, "for the good of human beings; [and action] that will eliminate the injustices."[148] The formulation did not have the old bite to it. Malcolm X sounded here very like a bland liberal, perhaps for the first time in his public career. In the end, it had all overwhelmed Malcolm X. He now stood between life and death, where few men stand to tell of it, and spoke to the society out of a frightening abyss. Malcolm X could not help complain of the burdens he had borne. Other men had spoken similar words.

> . . . . Had it pleased heaven
> To try me with affliction, had they rained
> All kinds of sores and shames on my bare head,
> Steeped me in poverty to the very lips,
> Given to captivity me and my utmost hopes,
> I should have found in some place of my soul
> A drop of patience. But, alas, to make me
> The fixed figure for the time of scorn
> To point his slow unmoving finger at.
> Yet could I bear that too; well, very well.
>
> (*Othello* IV, 2)

. . . 'Tis not so now.
. . . When we shall meet at compt,
This look of thine will hurl my soul from heaven,
And fiends will snatch at it. . . .

> O cursed, cursed slave! whip me, ye devils
> From the possession of this heavenly sight!
> Blow me about in winds! roast me in sulfur!
> Wash me in steep-down gulfs of liquid fire!
>
> *(Othello* V, 2)

Malcolm X had also fixed his eyes on the slave period and
identified, for the first time here, the cruelest kind of white
man in history. Again he was in the midst of powerful
beasts. No region of his mind seemed free of the memory
of slavery.

> . . . How could they make us slaves?
> They had to do the same thing to us that
> we do to a horse. When you take a horse out
> of the wilds, you don't just jump on him
> and ride him, or put a bit in his mouth
> and use him to plow with. No, you've got
> to break him in first. Once you break
> him in, then you can ride him. Now the
> man who rides him is not the man who breaks
> him in. It takes a different type of man
> to break him in than it takes to ride him.
> It takes a cruel man to break him in, a
> mean man, a heartless man, a man with
> no feelings.
>
> . . . If you find the role that that
> slave maker played, I'm telling you, you'll
> find it hard to forget and forgive, you'll
> find it hard.[149]

Yet, Malcolm X bore it all reasonably well for all that,
for all that. But most of what he drew from Negro history
and American society were archaic and cruel ideas, useless
things to calm a raging race war. The Negro did wish to be
stirred up by a vigorous and courageous voice. But being a

practical people, he also valued a good sense of direction. The Negro also wished desperately for a full racial pride. This was the only relevant legacy left by Malcolm X. But paradox appeared even here. Malcolm X left the Negro not only racial pride, but a certain arrogance that has now become the façade of an essentially rhetorical black nationalism.

VI. THE SETTING OF MALCOLM X'S EXILE

It is always difficult, to use the Negro folk idiom, to know where a man really "lives." What really matters to him? If he has come a distance in his life, over rough terrain, what of his past is still relevant and meaningful? The personal history of Malcolm X is as much the history of the setting of his life as the history of the inner man. Such a mixture of the personal and public always produces paradox. Malcolm X came from the dark underside of America. He said as much himself. But what did he bring with him to his stage, to the public platforms of America? He brought forward, stored in his mind and emotions, the three attitudes one expected to find in such a pugnacious, tough man: anger, insight, and honesty.

Malcolm X imagined that a dangerous white crowd surrounded Negro communities in the South and in the North. No Negro face appeared in the crowd. In Malcolm X's mind, white and Negro groups seldom met, except when a white chased a Negro back "across the tracks" or back to the "boulevard," or when a Negro

exacted retribution for the hideous crime of white racism.
As Malcolm X saw it, a Negro was indeed a man of another
people and another place. We should also imagine Malcolm X surrounded by a white crowd. But Malcolm X
actually saw much more around him. In his imagination,
he also saw the splendid, bright, wealthy, white suburban
communities of America. But the image of America
changed quickly from a bright image of wealth to an
image of a jungle. Malcolm X's image of America was
of a cold, bleak jungle populated by men wearing masks
of hatred, with cold hearts, cynical and sinister. All the
characters had now taken their places on Malcolm X's
stage of crime.

When the white crowd of America spoke, Malcolm X
heard the seemingly eternal hatred and fear of the Negro
by white men. Shakespeare begins his *Othello* with the
same predispositions. Shakespeare's characters would do
nicely for Malcolm X's white crowd. In his crowd's talk,
we are back to the world of animals and devils, back to
Malcolm X's bestiary. Roderigo and Iago warn Desdemona's father, Brabantio, that the mixing of the races is
against the law of nature and of civilized society. According
to Roderigo, Iago and Brabantio, the marriage of Desdemona and Othello will bring about the procreation of an
animal world. Such mixing has to be stopped.

IAGO: Rouse him. Make after him, poison his delight,
Proclaim him in the streets, incense her kinsmen,
And though he in a fertile climate dwell,
Plague him with flies. . . .

— — — — — — — — — — — — — — — — — —

RODERIGO: Sir,
Your daughter, if you have not given her leave,
I say again, hath made a gross revolt,

Tying her duty, beauty, wit, and fortunes
In a wondering and whelling stranger
Of here and everywhere. Straight satisfy yourself.
If she be in her chamber, or your house,
Let loose on me the justice of the state

For thus deluding you.

————————————————————

IAGO: . . . You'll have your daughter covered with a Barbary
horse, you'll have your grandsons neigh to you, you'll have
coursers for relations, and Spanish horses for relatives.

(Othello, I, 1)

Brabantio does not need more persuasion. He has already suspected that such dreadful things as these will happen if the black Othello continues to see his daughter. He
has already dreamed that such a thing as Iago had prophe-
sied has happened that very night. Brabantio is ready
to force Othello to leave Venice or to murder him. Brabantio calls up his crowd.

BRABANTIO: Strike on the tinder, ho!
Give me a taper! Call up my people!
This happening is not unlike my dream.
Belief of it oppresses me already.
Light, I say! Light!

(Othello, I, 1)

It does not matter that we are discussing the love affair
of Othello and Desdemona. Othello is also a play about
moral rectitude, power and cruelty; a play about how a
stranger fares in the grip of the mechanism of an alien
society. As such it is a play that sheds light on Malcolm X's
life and career. Malcolm X was also a stranger and a fugitive. Malcolm X's "cause" was to reconstruct and protect
the order of the fragile Negro world. Othello also keeps

secret the true place where he lives, the very meager foundations of his security and citizenship. Othello clings to his honor and honesty in love. His "cause" is to protect the order of this flimsy world.

Othello's reaction to Brabantio's crowd is revealed much later in the play. We discover he has indeed thought himself a stranger in Venice, and thus, finally, finds it easy to distrust Desdemona. But if Othello distrusts Desdemona, he also loves her. With her he loves the security she has given him with her love. It is the one secure thing he possesses in all of Venice. Othello speaks with great feeling about this. His admission of vulnerability marks a turning point in Shakespeare's play. A little later Othello will murder Desdemona and then murder himself. In Shakespeare, murder seems always to follow confrontation with the truth and with reality.

> OTHELLO: . . . There where I have garnered up my heart,
> Where either I must live or bear no life,
> The foundation from the which my current runs
> Or else dries up—to be discarded thence,
> Or keep it as a cistern for foul toads
> To knot and gender in—turn thy complexion there,
> Patience, thou young and rose-lipped cherubin!
> I here look grim as hell!
>
> *(Othello*, IV, 2)

Malcolm X looked "grim as hell." The security of the Negro race depended on his success in the radical Negro cause. The tenuous place of his security in America was in fact his stake in the independence of her Negro citizens.

Malcolm X's life and career can only be presented in the modern theater, not in a cozy, romantic Hollywood setting. The modern theater is void of lies. Life is twisted aright to portray reality. In the modern theater, and in

Shakespeare, life is a serious business; and so it was with Malcolm X. I have really imagined Malcolm X's life in the setting of Georg Büchner's *Woyzeck* as presented by the young American director John Lithgow in Cambridge, Massachusetts, several years ago. Here was a modern and cruel play. Lithgow used two platforms for *Woyzeck's* stage and a black backdrop. The floor of this stage was strewn with dirty rags, and perhaps with masks; or were they the heads of half-human creatures? When Lithgow's scenes were played on the two platforms, the setting of Woyzeck's world was a bare and simple wood structure.

But the backdrop to Malcolm X's stage must have a small sun painted on it; and more, it must really have stars and galaxies. The backdrop to Malcolm X's life was the supernatural world, the universe. The sun must be high to the left of Malcolm X's stage. For Malcolm X, the sun was the most important prop of his universe. If it fell, the world was out of order. When he was ostracized from the Black Muslim movement by Elijah Muhammad, he spoke of this sun: "I felt as though something in nature had failed," he wrote in his autobiography, "like the sun, or the stars."[150] In a way, the elements of the universe were analogous to the forces of history for Malcolm X. The elements were beyond his control, and he discovered finally that history was beyond his control. Woyzeck too is frightened of the elements of the universe. He also watches them to find a clue as to how he stands in the world and to discover which direction he should take to find supporters for his cause. Woyzeck watches the sun and also the ferocious animals about him; animals that are on the verge of attacking him and destroying the order of the world. Like Othello, Woyzeck thinks his moral rectitude upholds the moral order. Malcolm X held the same point of view. All our characters fear an empty sky.

MARIE: All these lights!
WOYZECK: Sure, Marie. Black cats with fiery eyes.
(Woyzeck, Scene V)

_ _ _ _ _ _ _ _ _ _ _ _ _ _ _ _

God, blow out the sun and let them roll on
    each other in their lechery.
(Woyzeck, Scene VII)

_ _ _ _ _ _ _ _ _ _ _ _ _ _ _

The world is out of order.
(Woyzeck, Scene XII)

_ _ _ _ _ _ _ _ _ _ _ _ _ _ _ _

OTHELLO: Are there not stones in heaven
But what serves for the thunder?

_ _ _ _ _ _ _ _ _ _ _ _ _ _ _ _

It is the cause, it is the cause, my soul.
Let me not name it to you, you chaste stars.
It is the cause.
(Othello, V, 2)

_ _ _ _ _ _ _ _ _ _ _ _ _ _ _

MALCOLM X: I thought something in nature had failed.

    Malcolm X saw society mirrored in the supernatural
world. At the beginning of his career, the universe and
society were under the control of Elijah Muhammad.
But Malcolm X was a curiously humble man. We do not
find in Malcolm X the arrogance of Herman Melville's
Ahab, who threatens to "strike the sun if it insulted" him.
Malcolm X did not think himself that tough and that
righteous. He adhered to a hierarchic and thus conservative view of the world. He was the subordinate of Elijah
Muhammad. When no longer a Black Muslim minister
he clung to the Negro cause as his lord and master. The
trouble was that the Negro cause was like a mirage before

him. It had to be defined more precisely, given coherence and shape; described for all time.

Malcolm X was very much the stranger in white America. America was a hostile place for him. He had, therefore, a somewhat impressionistic view of American society. He was unsure of the whites and unsure of the Negroes. Even when he addressed the white audiences of liberal American universities, he was suspicious of their intentions. Malcolm X's actual attitude toward whites was set forth in a Harlem speech and in a language that suited his bestiary. He wished to warn the Negro of white hypocrisy and violence. He repeated his instructions to the Negro audience, as if they would not really understand him.

MALCOLM X: You have to speak their language. The language that they were speaking . . . was the language of brutality. Beasts, they were, beating her. . . .
. . . He's talking the language of violence while you and I are running around with this little chicken-picking type of language.[151]

Malcolm X's genius was in knowing how to say such things. His speeches to white audiences, as in the Harvard speeches, were no less radical. His views gained a measure of quiet acceptance among some whites. In a curious way, whites respected Malcolm X, perhaps, mainly for his "straight talk" and for his great courage, and because he did not pretend to be a shining knight but had indeed come a great distance over rough terrain.

Robert Penn Warren gives Malcolm X credit for fighting his way to the top. But Warren's assessment of Malcolm X places too great an emphasis on his role as a hero and an American success story. Malcolm X had started out from the underside of American history; not, as Warren argues, from the place where the successful American hero had arisen in the past. Warren does not pay sufficient attention to the setting of Malcolm X's life and career and calls him a hero when he was really something altogether different. "Malcolm X," Warren argues, "was a latter-day example of an old-fashioned type of American celebrated in grammar school readers, commencement addresses, and speeches at Rotary Club luncheons—the man who 'makes it,' the man who, from humble origins and with meager education, converts, by will, intelligence and sterling character, his liabilities into assets." "Malcolm X," Warren continues, "was of that breed of Americans, autodidacts and homemade successes, that has included Benjamin Franklin, Abraham Lincoln, P. T. Barnum, Charles A. Edison, Booker T. Washington, Mark Twain, Henry Ford, and the Wright Brothers." Warren concludes: "Malcolm X would look back on his beginnings and, in innocent joy, marvel at the distance he had come."[152] Innocent joy? What a romantic explanation! If Malcolm X had found himself on the same stage with Warren's famous men, he would most certainly have gotten off it. He would have left such a stage dissenting from the legends of such heroes.

Malcolm X was not a hero. The underside of America did not produce such a romantic character. Any title given Malcolm X should not be romantic. Warren did not see a Horatio Alger story or a martyr, but a terrifying and fascinating stranger and fugitive. Warren saw a part of American history that had not yet been written. He actually saw a figure from the "other" American history— the dark underside filled with Negroes and the unimportant. The "other" American history had its own measurement of success, which included a fierce sense of integrity and a striking insight into the real nature of American society. From such a vantage point, it was a preoccupation to observe the rich and the powerful. The inhabitants of this sector of America are members of a natural, albeit flimsy, society forged with the will to survive and the wish to be wise about life in order, also, to survive. Malcolm X is best called an ordinary man; for even if he was brilliant and a genius he had learned his language, integrity, and courage in the streets and in the end owed his success to how he was received by the very special Negro sector of American society. That sector saw him as a prophet and rebel.

Malcolm X dedicated his life to the Negro cause. He might also have insisted that he had devoted himself to describing the actual Negro condition in America and to working for its improvement. Malcolm X's theory of Negro leadership was at once elitist and populist. The mass of folk loomed large in his public career and in his imagination. Yet he could not be a leader if he was not "his own man." The trouble with such attitudes toward leadership is that American society is filled with selfish and cruel people and one so easily stumbles into such dangerous situations. When disputes arose over leadership and ideology, there seemed only one way to settle such disagreements. The final solution governed Malcolm X's opponents' strategy. It all came down to a simple formula: "I win, you lose. Winner take all."

The sector of America from which Malcolm X had come does not produce shiny heroes. The Negro middle class has produced a bevy since the seventeenth century. The Negro lower class, which bears the brunt of white racism, has produced, instead, tough and largely inconspicuous rebels and prophets. Malcolm X was something of both. The prophet and rebel were most effective if they could exchange the past for the present. By some means, they thought, the Negro had to be given backbone. The prophet in Malcolm X reflected his interest in the secular world and in political power. To the Negro group, Malcolm X was mostly a rebel. In this role, he accomplished a great deal. The vantage point that must be assumed to appreciate his accomplishments is of the sector of society that idealizes the social outcast and the rebel. In this sector, ordinary ways of judging events are turned on their head. To lose is to win. It is also the case that actual accomplishments are not really required. The most pressing need of the members of such a sector is to have someone describe just what kind of world surrounds them. They also wish to know how far the group has come. What is the setting of their life? Thereafter, they seek an answer to a most secret and personal question: "If we are weak, are we courageous?" As a prophet of the Negro, Malcolm X wove a heroic myth of the Negro struggle. "You were once kings," he said. The rebel in him knew the great bulk of the Negro population faced near disaster year after year. Malcolm X constantly urged the Negro to look to the past where they had been cleansed by the cruelty of the slave institutions. He saw perfection in the Negro, if only because the Negro had a chance to be morally superior to the whites. And, in the end, perfection was always rewarded. Malcolm X knew what the white world offered the rebellious Negro. He had survived the prisons and now sought exile among men of his own kind and color. Through his intelligence, he had become conscious of the full horror of being Negro. He did not really care about reason, modernization, and political power. Malcolm X did not realize, however, how dangerous it was to attract people to the past. The legends of prophets also were an opiate of the masses. But Malcolm X was embittered. This was indeed the strongest emotion of his exile.

Throughout most of his life, Malcolm X thought him-

self confined to the Negro world. The canopy above him
here was the architecture of the Negro ghetto; the bare
wooden boards of shabby apartments and the old brown-
stone houses that were the hallmarks of the urban Negro
areas of the 1930's. It did not matter that Malcolm X had
lived a much more cosmopolitan life since becoming
Elijah Muhammad's national minister in 1961. Malcolm X
seemed to think he continued to live in the old setting of
his early adult life in Roxbury, Massachusetts, and in
Harlem, New York. The urban Negro crowds of the city
seemed to surround him or to fill his imagination even
when he was not on a platform before them or walking
along the streets of the ghetto. Malcolm X never forgot the
people and ideas of his past. Consequently, the actual social
setting of his exile was also a very personal world. It was
also a world, to follow Martin Kilson and James Wilson
at the second Harvard speech, full of tough realities and
built on a social structure weak of social pathology. The
Negro world in which Malcolm X lived and thought was
the underside of America.

The social setting of Malcolm X's exile was, of course,
at the threshold of existence of the poor Negro sector of
American society. I have, indeed, tried to map Malcolm
X's image of the social setting of this sector through an
analysis of his rhetoric and ideas. But what of the actual
place of his exile? The structure of the Negro sector as a
whole was really fourfold; and each sector seemed to en-
gender certain life chances and a certain view of life.

With Malcolm X, however, we must imagine ourselves
in the third sector of the Negro social structure, just above
what Karl Marx would have called the *lumpenproletariat.*
Malcolm X then was of the Negro "third element." The
third element of any industrial society contains people
anxious to improve themselves. Malcolm X sought to im-

prove his social position in various ways throughout his life. The constituency of the third element among the American Negro includes the loosely coherent group just below the middle class. On its illegal side it embraces the hustler society, and on the legal side the flimsy associations organized around the minimal social and economic interests of the Negro poor. At bottom, the strata includes the array of poor Negroes just inside the doors of organizations as well as, on many occasions, the members of crowds and mobs drawn to public events in hope of a strategy of survival and progress. The Negro third element really lives in a separate society. The interaction of this group with the larger society is actually very minimal.

The individual member of the Negro third element senses an isolation in Negro society because the strata is in limbo, neither coherent nor of the middle class or the lumpen group. The members of the group possess some talent, high inspiration and also, being deprived of racial equality, could thus be said to sense an exile of origin as well as an exile of place. The civil rights movement of Reverend Martin Luther King inspired a race consciousness among the third element in the South and North, starting in 1955, although this group did not comprise the bulk of King's supporters. The membership of the Black Muslim movement was precisely of this strata, and most of the ingenuity of the movement was derived from a very talented membership and hard-working tertiary elite. The isolation of the third element required a radical strategy, different in tone and goal from the strategy of the Negro middle class.

Malcolm X had urged his constituency and his crowds to follow a twofold strategy. He called for the use of politics and also urged rebellion. But Malcolm X did not call for politics as usual. It had to be done with a radical style.

In the heat of the moment, Malcolm X surely thought his strategy had carried the day. After his death, the student leaders stepped forward, center stage. The strategy they put forward is also clothed in tough rhetoric. The difference between the new leadership and Malcolm X is that the young leaders are Hamlets with books in their hands. To them, the radical Negro cause seems not really a serious and profound matter. It seems very much an idea for the moment, a strategy of anger. The new radical leadership has not traveled Malcolm X's distance over rough terrain. They appear, then, less humane and hesitant and thus prone to more hasty proposals.

It was likely that the dramatic leaders of the radical Negro cause would not secure the real, tangible progress the race had sought over a long, bleak history. The Negro situation required, as in *Hamlet,* that some other kind of leader come after a Hamlet. The prophet and rebel is always followed by the politician. As with Hamlet, so with Malcolm X and Stokely Carmichael and H. Rap Brown. Hamlet is followed by Fortinbras. Fortinbras will propose to do public and political things. Shakespeare's Fortinbras does not really say enough, and he says very polite and romantic things. But the Fortinbras of Zbigniew Herbert's modern poem gives a strategy of the private and public life that the best kind of leader must pursue. A Negro politician might deliver the elegy as comment on Malcolm X's life and career.

Elegy of Fortinbras

Now you have peace Hamlet you accomplished what you had to
and you have peace The rest is not silence but belongs to me
you chose the easier part an elegant thrust
But what is heroic death compared to eternal watching

with a cold apple in one's hand on a narrow chair
with a view on the ant-hill and the clock's dial

Adieu Prince I have tasks a sewer project
and a decree on prostitutes and beggars
I must also elaborate a better system of prisons
since as you justly said Denmark is a prison
I go to my own affairs This night was born
a star named Hamlet We shall never meet
what I will leave will not deserve tragedy
It is not for us to greet each other not bid farewell
and that water these words what can they do What can they do
                                                        Prince.[153]

Fortinbras does not propose a strategy of restraint. He is
simply less weighted down by history, less likely to be en-
trapped by the yoke that circumstance and history bestowed
on Hamlet. Malcolm X needs to be followed by the same
kind of leader. Fortinbras really supports a stoic and practical public policy; a politics of reconstruction—urgent
and permanent. Denmark will no longer be a place of exile,
but a seat of relevant, constructive power. The young may
then inherit a new mood and history a new direction.

PART TWO

THE HARVARD SPEECHES

THE HARVARD LAW
SCHOOL FORUM OF
MARCH 24, 1961[154]

Roger Fisher, Moderator

Mr. Malcolm X is a minister of Mosque No. 7, the Nation of Islam, Harlem, New York. Mr. X has agreed to speak to us on *The American Negro: Problems and Solutions.*

Malcolm X

We thank you for inviting us here to the Harvard Law School Forum this evening to present our views on this timely topic: *The American Negro: Problems and Solutions.* However, to understand our views, the views of the Muslims, you must first realize that we are a religious group, and you must also know something about our religion, the religion of Islam. The creator of the universe, whom many of you call God or Jehovah, is known to the Muslims by the name Allah. The Muslims believe there is but one God, and that all the prophets came from this one God. We believe also that all prophets taught the same religion, and that they themselves called that religion Islam, an Arabic word that means complete submission and obedience to the will of Allah. One who practices divine obedience is called a Muslim (commonly known, spelled, and referred to here in the West as Moslem). There are over seven hundred twenty-five million Muslims on this earth, predominantly in Africa and Asia, the nonwhite world. We here in America are under the divine leadership of the Honorable Elijah Muhammad, and we are an integral part of the vast world of Islam that stretches from the China seas to the sunny shores of West Africa. A unique situation faces the twenty million ex-slaves here in America because of our unique condition. Our acceptance of Islam and conversion to the religion affects us also in a unique way, different from the way in which it affects all other Muslin converts elsewhere on this earth.

Mr. Elijah Muhammad is our divine leader and teacher here in America. Mr. Muhammad believes in and obeys God one hundred percent, and he is even now teaching and working among our people to fulfill God's divine purpose. I am here at this forum tonight to represent Mr. Elijah Muhammad, the spiritual head of the fastest-growing group of Muslims in the Western Hemisphere. We who follow Mr. Muhammad know that he has been divinely taught and sent to us by God Himself. We believe that the miserable plight of the twenty million black people in America is the fulfillment of divine prophecy. We believe that the serious race problem that [the Negro's] presence here poses for America is also the fulfillment of divine prophecy. We also believe that the presence today in America of the Honorable Elijah Muhammad, his teachings among the twenty million so-called Negroes, and his naked warning to America concerning her treatment of these twenty million ex-slaves is also the fulfillment of divine prophecy. Therefore, when Mr. Muhammad declares that the only solution to America's serious race problem is complete separation of the two races, he is reiterating what was already predicted for this time by all the Biblical prophets. Because Mr. Muhammad takes this uncompromising stand, those of you who don't understand Biblical prophecy wrongly label him a racist and hate-teacher and accuse him of being anti-white and teaching black supremacy. But this evening since we are all here at the Harvard Law School Forum; together, both races face to face, we can question and examine for ourselves the wisdom or folly of what Mr. Muhammad is teaching.

Many of you who classify yourselves as white express surprise and shock at the truth that Mr. Muhammad is teaching your twenty million ex-slaves here in America, but you should be neither surprised nor shocked. As students, teachers, professors, and scientists, you should be well aware that we are living in a world where great changes are taking place. New ideas are replacing the old ones. Old governments are collapsing, and new nations are being born. The entire old system which held the old world together has lost its effectiveness, and now that old world is going out. A new system or a new world must replace the old world. Just as the old ideas must be removed to make way for the new, God has declared to Mr. Muhammad that the evil features of this wicked old world must be exposed, faced up to, and removed in order to make way for the new world which God Himself is preparing to establish. The divine mission of Mr. Muhammad here in America today is to prepare us for the new world of righteousness by teaching us a better understanding of the old world's defects. Thus we may come to agree that God must remove this wicked old world.

We see by reports in the daily press that even many of you who are scholars and scientists think that the message of Islam that is being preached here in America among your twenty million ex-slaves is new, or that it is something Mr. Muhammad himself has made up. Mr. Muhammad's religious message is not new. All of the scientists and prophets of old predicted that a man such as he, with such a doctrine or message, would make his appearance among us at a time as that in which we are living today. It is written too in your own scriptures that this prophetic figure would not be raised up from the midst of the educated class, but that God would make His choice from among the lowly, uneducated, downtrodden, oppressed masses, from among the lowest element of America's twenty million ex-slaves. It would be as in the days when God raised up Moses from among the lowly Hebrew slaves and [com]missioned him to separate his oppressed people from a slave master named Pharaoh. Moses found himself opposed by the scholars and scientists of that day, who are symbolically described in the Bible as "Pharaoh's magicians." Jesus himself, a lowly carpenter, was also [com]missioned by God to find his people, the "lost sheep," and to separate them from their Gentile enemies and restore them to their own nation. Jesus also found himself opposed by the scholars and scientists of his day, who are symbolically described in the Bible as "scribes, priests, and Pharisees." Just as the learned class of those days disagreed with and opposed both Moses and Jesus primarily because of their humble origin, Mr. Elijah Muhammad is today likewise being opposed by the learned, educated intellectuals of his own kind, because of [his] humble origin. These modern-day "magicians, scribes, and Pharisees" try to ridicule Mr. Muhammad by emphasizing the humble origin of him and his many followers.

Moses was raised up among his enslaved people at a time when God was planning to restore them to a land of their own where they could give birth to a new civilization, completely independent of their former slave masters. Pharaoh opposed God's plan and God's servant, so Pharaoh and his people were destroyed. Jesus was sent among his people at a time when God was planning to bring about another great change. The dispensation preached by Jesus two thousand years ago ushered in a new type of civilization, the

Christian civilization, better known as the Christian world. The Holy Prophet Muhammad (may the peace and blessing of Allah be upon him!) came six hundred years after Jesus with another dispensation that did not destroy or remove the Christian civilization, but which put a dent in it, a wound that has lasted even until today. Now, today, God has sent Mr. Elijah Muhammad among the downtrodden and oppressed so-called American Negroes to warn that God is again preparing to bring about another great change, only this time it will be a final change. This is the day and the time for a complete change. Mr. Muhammad teaches that the religion of Islam is the only solution to the problems confronting our people here in America. He warns us that it is even more important, however, to know the base or foundation upon which we must build tomorrow. Therefore, although the way in which Mr. Muhammad teaches the religion of Islam and the particular kind of Islam he teaches may appear to be different from the teaching of Islam in the Old World, the basic principles and practices are the same.

You must remember: The condition of America's twenty million ex-slaves is uniquely pitiful. But just as the old religious leaders in the days of Moses and Jesus refused to accept Moses and Jesus as religious reformers, many of the religious leaders in the old Muslim world today may also refute the teachings of Mr. Elijah Muhammad, neither realizing the unique condition of these twenty million ex-slaves nor understanding that Mr. Elijah Muhammad's teachings are divinely prescribed to rectify the miserable condition of our oppressed people here. But as God made Pharaoh's magicians bow before Moses, and the scribes and Pharisees bow before Jesus, He plans today to make all opposition, both at home and abroad, bow before the truth that is now being taught by the Honorable Elijah Muhammad.

We are two thousand years from the time of the great

change which took place in Jesus' day. If you will but look around you on this earth today, it will be as clear as the five fingers on your hand that we are again living at a time of great change. God has come to close out the entire old world, the old world where for the past six thousand years most of the earth's population has been deceived, conquered, colonized, ruled, enslaved, oppressed, and exploited by the Caucasian race. At the time when Pharaoh's civilization reached its peak and his period of rule of the slaves was up, God appeared unto Moses and revealed to him that He had something different for his people. Likewise, God told Mr. Muhammad that He has something different for his people, the so-called Negroes here in America today—something that until now has never before been revealed. Mr. Muhammad teaches us that this old world has seen nothing yet, that the real thing is yet to come.

The Black Muslims who follow Mr. Muhammad are only now making their exit from the old world. The door to the new world is yet to be opened, and what is inside that door is yet to be revealed. The teaching of Mr. Muhammad among your twenty million ex-slaves is only to prepare us to walk out of this wicked old world in as intelligent, pleasant, and peaceful a way as possible. The teaching among the so-called American Negroes is designed only to show proof why we should give up this wicked old house. The roof is leaking, the walls are collapsing, and we find it can no longer support the tremendous weight caused by our continued presence in it. The knowledge of the deterioration and eventual collapse of this old building having come to Mr. Muhammad from Almighty God Himself (whose proper name is Allah, the Lord of all the worlds, the Master of Judgment Day), the Honorable Elijah Muhammad is pointing out these dangerous conditions and

future results to us as well as to you who have enslaved us.
With proper support and guidance our people can get out
of this sagging old building before it collapses. But the
support and guidance that we need actually consists of instruction in the origin, history, and nature of the Caucasian
race as well as of our own black nation. We must have a
thorough knowledge of the true origin and history of the
white man's Christian religion as well as an understanding
of the Islamic religion that prevails primarily among our
brothers and sisters in Africa and Asia. You will probably
ask us, "Why, if this old house is going to collapse or go up
in smoke, are the Black Muslims asking for some states to
be set aside in this country? It's like asking for a chance to
retain rooms in a house that you claim is doomed for total
destruction!"

God is giving to America every opportunity to repent
and atone for the crime she committed when she enslaved
our people, even as God gave Pharaoh a chance to repent
before He finally destroyed that king, too proud to face his
slaves and give them complete justice. We are asking you
for a territory here only because of the great opposition we
receive from this government in our efforts to awaken our
people, to unite them and separate them from their oppres-
sors, and to return them to their own land and people. You
should never make the mistake of thinking that Mr. Muhammad has no place to take his followers in the World of
Islam. No sir! He is not shut out from the world as many
of you wish to believe. All who accept Islam and follow Mr.
Muhammad have been offered a home in the Muslim
world.

Our people have been oppressed and exploited here in
America for four hundred years, and now with Mr. Muhammad we can leave this wicked world of bondage. But
our former slave master is [continually] opposing Mr. Mu-

hammad's efforts and is unjustly persecuting those who have left the Christian Church and accepted the religion of Islam. This is further proof that our Caucasian slave master does not want or trust us to leave him and live elsewhere on this earth. And yet, if we stay here with him, he continues to keep us at the very lowest level of his society.

Pick up any daily newspaper or magazine and examine the anti-Muslim propaganda and the false charges leveled against our beloved religious leader by some of America's leading reporters. This only points up the fact that the Caucasian race is never willing to let any black man who is not their puppet or parrot speak for our people or lead our people out of their enslaving clutches without giving him great opposition. The Caucasian slave master has opposed all such leaders in the past, and even today he sanctions and supports only those Negro spokesmen who parrot his doctrines and ideas or who accept his so-called advice on how our people should carry on our struggle against his four hundred years of tyranny.

The Christian world has failed to give the black man justice. The [American] Christian government has failed to give her twenty million ex-slaves [just compensation] for three hundred ten years of free slave labor. Even despite this, we have been better Christians than those who taught us Christianity. We have been America's most faithful servants during peace time, and her bravest soldiers during war time. But still, white Christians have been unwilling to recognize us and to accept us as fellow human beings. Today we can see that the Christian religion of the Caucasian race has failed us. Thus the black masses are turning away from the Church and toward the religion of Islam. Furthermore, the government sends its agents among our people to tell lies. [Those agents] make an all-out effort to harass us in order to frighten those of our people in this country who would accept the religion of Islam and unite under the spiritual guidance and divine leadership of the Honorable Elijah Muhammad. Therefore, Mr. Muhammad has demanded that you and your government let us separate ourselves from you right here, into a separate territory that we can call our own and on which we can do something for ourselves and for our own kind; since you don't want these twenty million ex-slaves to leave you and return to their own land and people, and since your actions have proved that the Caucasian race will not receive them as complete equals. Since we cannot live among the Caucasians in peace, and since there is not time enough for us new Negroes to wait for the Caucasian race to be "re-educated" and freed of their racial prejudice, their inbred beliefs and practices of white supremacy, I repeat, "Let our people be separated from you, and give us some territory that we can call our own and where we can live in peace among ourselves."

According to recent news dispatches in daily papers throughout the nation, prison wardens all over this country are unjustly persecuting the inmates who want to change from the Christian religion to the religion of Islam and follow the spiritual guidance of the Honorable Elijah Muhammad. Indeed, these prison wardens even admit that when inmates change from Christianity to Islam, they become model prisoners. Yet despite this, the prisoners are being persecuted and prevented from reading the Holy Koran, the same holy book that is read daily by hundreds of millions of our darker brothers and sisters in Africa and Asia. When the true facts about this religious persecution are made known among the seven hundred twenty-five million Muslims in the world of Islam, that strategic area that stretches from the China seas to the shores of West Africa, how do you think the American Caucasians will then look

in the eyes of those nonwhite people there? The very fact
that there is a concerted effort against Islam by prison wardens in this country is proof that the American government
is trying to stamp out the religion of Islam at home, in a
frantic effort to keep it from spreading among her twenty
million ex-slaves whom she continues to confine to the
lowly role of second-class citizenship. Further proof is the
fact that these twenty million so-called Negroes have never
been taught about the religion of Islam during the entire
four hundred years, since the Caucasians first brought our
people here in chains from our African Muslim culture.
Yet Islam is, and always has been, the prevailing religion
among our people in Africa. Indeed, the American Caucasian, in a last act of desperation, is accusing Mr. Muhammad of not being a true Muslim, and of not teaching true
Islam. If the American Caucasian knows so much about
true Islam and has suddenly become such an authority on
it, why hasn't he taught it to his twenty million ex-slaves
before now?

The American Caucasian today also loves to print glar-
ing headlines saying that the orthodox Muslims don't recognize or accept Mr. Muhammad and his Muslims as true
Muslims. "Divide and rule" has long been the Caucasian
strategy to continue white colonization of dark nations.
The American Caucasian actually has settled twenty million black people here in this country by simply dividing
us from our African brothers and sisters for four hundred
years, converting us to his Christian religion, and by teaching us to call ourselves "Negroes" and telling us that we
are no longer African. (I guess he says this because our ex-
posure to this "superior" white culture makes us different,
so-called civilized.) Since hundreds of thousands of the ex-
slaves here in America today refuse to attend the church of
the Caucasians who enslaved us, shun all further use of the

word "Negro," and accept Allah as their God, Islam as their religion, and the Honorable Elijah Muhammad as their religious leader and teacher, these American Caucasians are reverting to the old trick of earlier colonialists: divide and rule. They thereby try to separate us from the Muslim world and to alienate us from our people in Africa and Asia who also serve and follow Almighty God, Allah.

There are probably one hundred thousand of what you (whites) call orthodox Muslims in America, who were born in the Muslim world and who willingly migrated here. But despite the fact that Islam is a propagating religion, all of these foreign Muslims combined have not been successful in converting one thousand Americans to Islam. On the other hand, they see that Mr. Muhammad by himself has hundreds of thousands of his fellow ex-slaves turning eastward toward Mecca five times daily giving praises to the great God Allah. No true Muslim in his right mind would denounce or deny this meek and humble little black man, born in Georgia in the very worst part of this country, as a leader, a defender of the faith, and a propagator of the faith, who has rekindled the light of Islam here in the West. His Caucasian opposers have never gotten even one responsible Muslim official to criticize or denounce Mr. Muhammad. They succeed only in getting some jealous, envious little peddler or merchant who migrated here and who wants to be recognized as some sort of leader himself and will therefore accept the Caucasian's bribe of thirty pieces of silver to attack this man of God. How could Mr. Muhammad ever make a trip into the forbidden areas of Arabia, to visit the holy cities of Mecca and Medina, and be welcomed and honored by its most respected religious leaders, the great Imams themselves, if he himself were not recognized as a great religious man, a man of God, doing miraculous works by spreading Allah's name here in the

West among the twenty million ex-slaves of America? How could Mr. Muhammad visit the capitals of the Muslim world and be received by its respected leaders, if he were not also recognized and respected as a Muslim leader by them? He visited Al-Azhar, the oldest mosque and Muslim university in the world, and had tea with the Chief Imam, the Grand Sheikh Shaltuat, who kissed him on his forehead in true Muslim fashion. Yet the American Caucasians, hoping to block his success among our people, continue to oppose him and to say that he is not a true Muslim.

Again you will say, "Why don't he and his followers leave this house of bondage right now and go and live in the Muslim world?" All of the Nation of Islam can live in the Muslim world tomorrow, but the Honorable Elijah Muhammad wants justice for the entire twenty million so-called Negroes. You and your Christian government make the problem even more complicated. You don't want your twenty million ex-slaves to leave you, yet you won't share equal justice with them right here. Since you don't want them to leave this country with us, and you won't give them equal justice among your kind, we will agree to stay only if you let us separate ourselves from you right here. Just give us a portion of this country that we can call our own. Put us in it. Then give us everything we need to start our own civilization—that is, support us for twenty to twenty-five years, until we are able to go for ourselves. This is God's plan. This is God's solution. This is justice, and compensation for our three hundred ten years of slave labor. Otherwise America will reap the full fury of God's wrath for her crimes against our people, which are many. As your Bible says, "He that leads into captivity shall go into captivity; he that kills with the sword shall be killed by the sword." This is the law of justice; this is in your own Christian scriptures.

The black masses are shaking off the drugs, the narcotic effect of token-integration promises. A cup of tea in a white restaurant is not sufficient compensation for three hundred ten years of free slave labor. The black masses as represented by the Black Muslims will never be satisfied until we have some land that we can call our own. Again I repeat: We are not asking for territory here because Mr. Muhammad has no place else to take us. But we ask for the sake of the entire twenty million so-called Negroes, twenty million ex-slaves who, despite the fact that the Emancipation Proclamation was issued one hundred years ago, are still begging their former slave master for recognition as human beings. Mr. Muhammad is asking this government to stop toying with our people, to stop fooling them year in and year out with false promises of token integration. Token integration will not solve our problem. This is a false solution, a "token" solution. It is a hypocritical approach to the problem, a tricky scheme devised by you and propagated by your Negro puppets whom you yourselves have appointed as our leaders and spokesmen.

Integration is not good for either side. It will destroy your race, and your government knows it will also destroy ours, and the problem still remains unsolved. God has declared that these twenty million ex-slaves must have a home of their own. After four hundred years here among the Caucasians, we are absolutely convinced that we can never live together in peace, unless we are willing to remain subservient to our former masters. Therefore, immediate and complete separation is the only solution. NAACP Attorney Thurgood Marshall has admitted publicly that six years since the Supreme Court decision on desegregation of the schools, only six percent desegregation has taken place. This is an example of integration!

A kidnapper, a robber, an enslaver, a lyncher is just another common criminal in the sight of God, and criminal acts as such have been committed by your race on a mass scale for four hundred years against your twenty million so-called Negroes. It is true that today America professes to be sorry for her crimes against our people. She says she wants to repent, but in her desire to atone or make amends, she offers her twenty million ex-slaves flowery promises of token integration. Many of these downtrodden victims want to forgive America. They want to forget the crimes that you have comitted against them, and some are even willing to accept the formula of token integration that you yourselves have devised as a solution to the problem created by your own criminal acts against them. In a court of justice the criminal can confess his crimes and throw himself on the mercy of the court if he truly repents, but neither the criminal nor his victim has any say-so in suggesting the sentence that is to be passed upon the guilty or the price that the confessed criminal must pay. This is left in the hands of the judge. We are living in the Day of Judgment right now. God is the Judge that our American slave master must now answer to. God is striking this country with tornadoes, storms, floods, rain, hail, snow; and terrific earthquakes are yet to come. Your people are being afflicted with increasing epidemics of illness, disease, and plagues, with which God is striking you because of your criminal acts against the twenty million ex-slaves.

Instead of repenting and truly compensating our people for their three hundred ten years of free slave labor that built up this country for you, you buy out the Negro leaders with thirty pieces of silver and have them sell our people your token integration. When one uses a token on the bus or streetcar, that token is a substitute for the real money; token means a substitute, that which takes the place of the real thing. Token integration takes the place of the real thing. Two black students at the University of Georgia is token integration. Four black children in New Orleans' white schools is token integration. A handful of black students in the white schools in Little Rock, Arkansas is token integration. None of this is real integration; it is only a pacifier to keep these awakening black babies from crying too loud. According to the above-mentioned rate of desegregation since the decision of the Supreme Court, it will take us another thousand years to get the white man in the South sufficiently "re-educated" to accept our people in their midst as equals. And if the rest of the truth is told, it will take the white man here in the North, West, and East just as long as his brother in the South.

To many of you here at the Harvard Law School Forum this sounds ridiculous; to some it even sounds insane. But these twenty million black people here in America now number a nation in their own right. Do you believe that a nation within another nation can be successful, especially when they both have equal educations? Once the slave has his master's education, the slave wants to be like his master, wants to share his master's property, and even wants to exercise the same privileges as his master while he is yet in his master's house. This is the core of America's troubles today: there will be no peace for America as long as twenty million so-called Negroes are here begging for the rights which America knows she will never grant us. The limited education America has granted her ex-slaves has even already produced great unrest. Almighty God says the only way for America to ever have any future or prosperity is for her twenty million ex-slaves to be separated from her, and it is for this reason that Mr. Muhammad teaches us that we must have some land of our own. If we receive equal education, how long do you expect us to remain your passive servants, or second-class citizens? There is no such thing as a second-class citizen. We are full citizens, or we are not citizens at all. When you teach a man the science of government, he then wants an equal part or position in that government, or else he wants his own government. He begins to demand equality with his master. No man with education equal to your own will serve you. The only way you can continue to rule us is with superior knowledge, by continuing to withhold equal education from our people. America has not given us equal education, but she has given us enough to make us want more and to make us demand equality of opportunity. And since this is causing unrest plus international embarrassment, the only solution is immediate separation. As your colleges and universities turn out an ever-increasing number of so-called Negro graduates with education equal to yours, they will automatically increase their demands for equality in everything else. Equal education will increase their spirit of equality and make them feel that they should have everything that you have, and their increasing demands will become a perpetual headache for you and continue to cause you international embarrassment. In fact, those Negro students whom you are educating today will soon be demanding the same things you now hear being demanded by Mr. Muhammad and the Muslims.

In concluding, I must remind you that your own Christian Bible states that God is coming in the last days or at the end of the old world, and that God's coming will bring about a great separation. Now since we see all sorts of signs throughout the earth that indicate that the time of God's coming is upon us, why don't you repent while there is yet time? Do justice by your faithful ex-slaves. Give us some land of our own right here, some separate states, so we can separate ourselves from you. Then everyone will be satisfied, and perhaps we will all be able to then live happily ever after and, as your own Christian Bible says, "everyone under his own vine and fig tree." Otherwise all of you who are sitting here, your government, and your entire race will be destroyed and removed from this earth by Almighty God, Allah.

THE LEVERETT HOUSE FORUM OF MARCH 18, 1964[155]

Archie Epps, Moderator

Academicians and laymen have often thought of Negro radicalism or nationalism in terms of pathology. In other words, Negro personalities in radical movements are thought to be abnormal, or shysters, or freaks of some sort. Accordingly, Negro radicalism is conceived of as the fervent product of systematic and protracted frustration; its ideology, a pathological response to economic, social, and cultural discrimination. The Negro radical movement is never credited with meaning what it says. Its pronouncements are interpreted rather than heard. None of its arguments is accorded the courtesy one gives reality. They are tolerated as the angry response of Negroes to white rejection. It is perhaps more nearly correct that what is often thought absurd about Negro radicalism turns out to be logical conclusions to a line of reasoning and experience which are unknown and beyond the imagination of most observers who are not themselves Negro. Negro radicalism is, rather, the spontaneous and articulated answer of some Negroes to real problems little appreciated by timid and peaceful souls.

It is nearer the truth, no doubt, that some of you have come to see and hear Malcolm X only to observe what you think is his curious pathology. Surely some have come for the reason one would attend a circus—to watch the dancing bear. To be sure, revolutions, and this one, are full of the inadequacies of men and of their pathologies; but, on the other hand, revolutions give rise to profound meditation on the problem of evil and on the place of man in society. Specifically, revolutions demonstrate in the clamor of men the economic forces of the age; their molding of society and politics, of men in the mass and individual man; and the powerful reaction of all these forces on the social environment at one of those rare moments when society is at a boiling point, fluid and therefore discernible to man. The conflicts of this revolutionary age in America enable us, I think, to see the very bones of American society. And it is no doubt incumbent on students and academicians, indeed, on all men to reconsider Negro radicalism, Negro movements, and all social history in light of discovering the social reality which is contained in them.

The speaker this evening is Mr. Malcolm X, who lives in New York State and is at this time Minister of Moslem Mosque, Incorporated.

Malcolm X

Nineteen hundred sixty-four will probably be the most explosive year that America has yet witnessed on the racial front; primarily because the black people of this country during 1963 saw nothing but failure behind every effort they made to get what the country was supposedly on record for. Today the black people in this country have become frustrated, disenchanted, disillusioned and probably more set for action now than ever before—not the kind of action that has been set out for them in the past by some of their supposedly liberal white friends, but the kind of action that will get some kind of immediate results. As the moderator has pointed out, the time that we're living in now and that we are facing now is not an era where one who is oppressed is looking toward the oppressor to give him some system or form of logic or reason. What is logical to the oppressor isn't logical to the oppressed. And what is reason to the oppressor isn't reason to the oppressed. The black people in this country are beginning to realize that what sounds reasonable to those who exploit us doesn't sound reasonable to us. There just has to be a new system of reason and logic devised by us who are at the bottom, if we want to get some results in this struggle that is called "the Negro revolution."

Not only is it going to be an explosive year on the racial front; it is going to be an explosive year on the political front. This year it will be impossible to separate one from the other. The politicking of the politicians in 1964 will probably do more to bring about racial explosion than any other factor, because this country has been under the rule of the politicians. When they want to get elected to office they come into the so-called Negro community and make a lot of promises that they don't intend to keep. This feeds the hopes of the people in our community, and after the politicians have gotten what they are looking for, they turn their back on the people of our community. This has happened time and time again. The only difference between then and now is that there is a different element in the community; whereas in the past the people of our community were patient and polite, long-suffering and willing to listen to what *you* call reason, 1964 has produced an element of people who are no longer willing to listen to what you call reason. As I said, what's reasonable to you has long since ceased to be reasonable to us. And it will be these false promises made by the politicians that will bring about the BOOM.

During the few moments that I have I hope that we can chat in an informal way, because I find that when you are discussing things that are very "touchy," sometimes it's best to be informal. And where white people are concerned, it has been my experience that they are extremely intelligent on most subjects until it comes to race. When you get to the racial issue in this country, the whites lose all their intelligence. They become very subjective, and they want to tell us how it should be solved. It's like Jesse James going to tell the Marshal how he should come after him for the crime that Jesse committed.

I am not a politician. I'm not even a student of politics. I'm not a Democrat. I'm not a Republican. I don't even consider myself an American. If I could consider myself an American, we wouldn't even have any problem. It would be solved. Many of you get indignant when you hear a black man stand up and say, "No, I'm not an American." I see whites who have the audacity, I should say the nerve, to think that a black man is radical and extremist, subversive and seditious if he says, "No, I'm not an American." But at the same time, these same whites have to admit that this man has a problem.

I don't come here tonight to speak to you as a Democrat or a Republican or an American or anything that *you* want me to be. I'm speaking as what I am: one of twenty-two million black people in this country who are victims of your democratic system. They're the victims of the Democratic politicians, the victims of the Republican politicians. They're actually the victims of what you call democracy. So I stand here tonight speaking as a victim of what you call democracy. And you can understand what I'm saying if you realize it's being said through the mouth of a victim; the mouth of one of the oppressed, not through the mouth and eyes of the oppressor. But if you think we're sitting in the same chair or standing on the same platform, then you won't understand what I'm talking about. You'd expect me to stand up here and say what you would say if you were standing up here. And I'd have to be out of my mind.

Whenever one is viewing this political system through the eyes of a victim, he sees something different. But today these twenty-two million black people who are the victims of American democracy, whether you realize it or not, are viewing your democracy with new eyes. Yesterday our people used to look upon the American system as an American dream. But the black people today are beginning to realize that it is an American nightmare. What is a dream to you is a nightmare to us. What is hope to you has long since become hopeless to our people. And as this attitude develops, not so much on Sugar Hill [in Harlem]—although it's there too—but in the ghetto, in the alley where the masses of our people live . . . there you have a new situation on your hands. There's a new political consciousness developing among our people in this country. In the past, we weren't conscious of the political maneuvering that goes on in this country, which exploits our people politically. We knew something was wrong, but we weren't conscious of what it was. Today there's a tendency on the part of this new generation of black people (who have been born and are growing up in this country) to look at the thing not as they wish it were, but as it actually is. And their ability to look at the situation as it is, is what is primarily responsible for the ever-increasing sense of frustration and hopelessness that exists in the so-called Negro community today.

Besides becoming politically conscious, you'll find that our people are also becoming more aware of the strategic position that they occupy politically. In the past, they weren't. Just the right to vote was considered something. But today the so-called Negroes are beginning to realize that they occupy a very strategic position. They realize what the new trends are and all of the new political tendencies.

During recent years at election time, when the Governor was running for office, there was call for a recount of votes here in Massachusetts. In Rhode Island it was the same way—in Minnesota, the same thing. Within American politics there is now such a similarity between the two parties that in elections the race is usually close enough to permit almost any single block to swing it one way or the other. Not only is this true in city, county, and state elections, but it's also true in the national elections, as witness the close race between President Kennedy and Nixon a few years back. And everyone admits that it was the strategic vote of the so-called Negro in this country that put the Kennedy administration in Washington. The position in the political structure of the so-called Negro has become so strategic that whenever any kind of election rolls around now, the politicians are out there trying to win the Negro vote. In trying to win the Negro vote, they make a whole lot of promises and build up his hopes. But they always build him up for a letdown. By being constantly built up for a letdown, the Negro is now becoming very angry at the white man. And in his anger the Muslims come along and talk to him. Yet instead of the white man blaming himself for the anger of the Negro, he again has the audacity to blame us. When we warn you how angry the Negro is becoming, you, instead of thanking us for giving you a little warning, try to accuse us of stirring up the Negro. Don't you know that if your house is on fire and I come to warn you that your house is burning, you shouldn't accuse me of setting the fire! Thank me rather for letting you know what's happening, or what's going to happen, before it's too late.

When these new trends develop in the so-called Negro in America, making the so-called Negro aware of his strategic position politically, he becomes aware too of what he's not getting in return. He realizes that his vote puts the governor in office, or the mayor in office, or the president in office. But he's beginning to see also that although his vote is the vital factor that determines who will sit in these seats, the last one those politicians try to help is the so-called Negro.

Proof of which: Everyone admits that it was the Negro vote that put Kennedy in the White House. Yet four years have passed and the present administration is just now getting around to civil rights legislation. In its fourth year of office it finally passes some kind of civil rights legislation, designed supposedly to solve the problem of the so-called Negro. Yet that voting element offered decisive support in the national election. I only cite this to show the hypocrisy on the part of the white man in America, whether he be down South or whether he be up here in the North.

Democrats, now after they've been in the White House awhile, use an alibi for not having kept their promise to the Negroes who voted for them. They say, "Well, we can't get this passed or we can't get that passed." The present make-up of the Congress is 257 Democrats and only 177 Republicans. Now how can a party of Democrats that received practically the full support of the so-called Negroes of this country and control nearly two-thirds of the seats in Congress give the Negro an excuse for not getting some kind of legislation passed to solve the Negro problem? Where the senators are concerned, there are 67 Democrats and only 33 Republicans; yet these Democrats are going to try to pass the buck to the Republicans after the Negro has put the Democrats in office. Now I'm not siding with either Democrats or Republicans. I'm just pointing out the deceit on the part of both when it comes to dealing with the Negro. Although the Negro vote put the Democratic Party where it is, the Democratic Party gives the Negro nothing; and the Democrats offer as an excuse that the fault lies with the Dixie-crats. What do you call them—Dixie-crats or Dixo-crats or Demo-Dixo-crats!

Look at the shrewd deceptive manner in which they deal with the Negro. A Dixo-crat is a Democrat. You can call them by whatever name you wish, but you have never seen a situation where the Dixie-crats kick the Democrats out of the party. Rather the Democrats kick the Dixie-crats out of their party if there is ever any cleavage. You oftentimes find the Dixie-crats "cussing out" the Democrats, but you never find the Democrats disassociating themselves from the Dixie-crats. They are together and they use this shrewd maneuvering to trick the Negro. Now there are some young Negroes appearing on the scene, and it is time for those who call themselves Democrats to realize that when the Negro looks at a Democrat, he sees a Democrat. Whether you call him a Dixo-Democrat or a Demo-Dixie-crat, he's the same thing.

One of the reasons that these Dixie-crats occupy such a powerful position in Washington, D.C., is that they have seniority. By reason of their seniority and primarily because they have denied the local Negro his right to vote, they hold sway over key committees in Washington. You call it a system based on democracy, yet you can't deny that the most powerful men in this government are from the South. The only reason they're in positions of power is because the Negroes in their area are deprived of their constitutional right to vote. But the Constitution says that when at any time the people of a given area are denied their right to vote, the representatives of that area are supposed to be expelled from their seat. You don't need any new legislation; it's right in front of you already. The only reason the politicians want new legislation is to use it to further trick the Negro. All they have to do is to go by that thing they call the Constitution. It needs no more bills, it needs no more amendments, it needs no more anything. All it needs is a little sincere application.

As with the South, the North knows its own by-pass for the Constitution, which goes by the name of "gerrymandering." Some fellows gain control in the so-called Negro community and then change voting lines every time the Negro begins to get too powerful numerically. The technique is different from that in Mississippi. There is no denying the Negro the right to vote outright, as in Mississippi. The Northern way is more shrewd and subtle; but whether victim of the Northern way or the Southern method, the Negro ends up with no political power whatsoever. Now, I may not be putting this in language which you're used to, but I'm quite sure that you get the point. Whenever you give the Negro in the South the right to vote, his Constitutional right to vote, it will mean an automatic change in the entire representation from the South. Were he able to exercise his right, some of the most powerful and influential figures in Washington, D.C., would not now be in the Capitol. A large Negro vote would change the foreign policy as well as the domestic policy of this government. Therefore the only valid approach toward revolutionizing American policy is to give to the Negro his right to vote. Once that is done, the entire future course of things must change.

I might say this is how we look at it—how the victims look at it, a very crude and what you might call pessimistic

view. But I should rather prefer it as a realistic view. Now
what is our approach towards solving this? Many of you
have probably just recently read that I am no longer an
active member in the Nation of Islam, although I am myself still a Muslim. My religion is still Islam, and I still
credit the Honorable Elijah Muhammad with being responsible for everything I know and everything that I am.
In New York we have recently founded the Muslim
Mosque, Incorporated, which has as its base the religion
of Islam, the religion of Islam because we have found that
this religion creates more unity among our people than
any other type of philosophy can do. At the same time, the
religion of Islam is more successful in eliminating the vices
that exist in the so-called Negro community, which destroy
the moral fiber of the so-called Negro community.

So with this religious base, the difference between the
Muslim Mosque, Incorporated, and the Nation of Islam is
probably this: We have as our political philosophy, Black
Nationalism; as our economic philosophy, Black Nationalism; and as our social philosophy, Black Nationalism. We
believe that the religion of Islam combined with Black
Nationalism is all that is needed to solve the problem that
exists in the so-called Negro community. Why?

The only real solution to our problem, just as the Honorable Elijah Muhammad has taught us, is to go back to
our homeland and to live among our own people and develop it so we'll have an independent nation of our own.
I still believe this. But that is a long-range program. And
while our people are getting set to go back home, we have
to live here in the meantime. So in the Honorable Elijah
Muhammad's long-range program, there's also a short-
range program: the political philosophy which teaches us
that the black man should control the politics of his own
community. When the black man controls the politics

and the politicians in his own community, he can then make them produce what is good for the community. For when a politician in the so-called Negro community is controlled by a political machine outside, seldom will that politician ever do what is necessary to bring up the standard of living or to solve the problems that exist in that community. So our political philosophy is designed to bring together the so-called Negroes and to re-educate them to the importance of politics in concrete betterment, so that they may know what they should be getting from their politicians in addition to a promise. Once the political control of the so-called Negro community is in the hands of the so-called Negro, then it is possible for us to do something towards correcting the evils and the ills that exist there.

Our economic philosophy of Black Nationalism means that instead of our spending the rest of our lives begging the white man for a job, our people should be re-educated to the science of economics and the part that it plays in our community. We should be taught just the basic fundamentals: that whenever you take money out of the neighborhood and spend it in another neighborhood, the neighborhood in which you spend it gets richer and richer, and the neighborhood from which you take it gets poorer and poorer. This creates a ghetto, as now exists in every so-called Negro community in this country. If the Negro isn't spending his money downtown with what we call "the man," "the man" is himself right in the Negro community. All the stores are run by the white man, who takes the money out of the community as soon as the sun sets. We have to teach our people the importance of where to spend their dollars and the importance of establishing and owning businesses. Thereby we can create employment for ourselves, instead of having to wait to boycott your stores and businesses to demand that you give us a job. Whenever the majority of our people begin to think along such lines, you'll find that we ourselves can best solve our problems. Instead of having to wait for someone to come out of your neighborhood into our neighborhood to tackle these problems for us, we ourselves may solve them.

The social philosophy of Black Nationalism says that we must eliminate the vices and evils that exist in our society, and that we must stress the cultural roots of our forefathers, that will lend dignity and make the black man cease to be ashamed of himself. We have to teach our people something about our cultural roots. We have to teach them something of their glorious civilizations before they were kidnapped by your grandfathers and brought over to this country. Once our people are taught about the glorious civilization that existed on the African continent, they won't any longer be ashamed of who they are. We will reach back and link ourselves to those roots, and this will make the feeling of dignity come into us; we will feel that as we lived in times gone by, we can in like manner today. If we had civilizations, cultures, societies, and nations hundreds of years ago, before you came and kidnapped us and brought us here, so we can have the same today. The restoration of our cultural roots and history will restore dignity to the black people in this country. Then we shall be satisfied in our own social circles; then we won't be trying to force ourselves into your social circles. So the social philosophy of Black Nationalism doesn't in any way involve any anti-anything. However, it does restore to the man who is being taunted his own self-respect. And the day that we are successful in making the black man respect himself as much as he now admires you, he will no longer be breathing down your neck every time you go buy a house somewhere to get away from him.

That is the political, social, and economic philosophy of

Black Nationalism, and in order to bring it about, the program that we have in the Muslim Mosque, Incorporated, places an accent on youth. We are issuing a call for students across the country, from coast to coast, to launch a new study of the problem—not a study that is in any way guided or influenced by adults, but a study of their own. Thus we can get a new analysis of the problem, a more realistic analysis. After this new study and more realistic analysis, we are going to ask those same students (by students I mean young people, who having less of a stake to lose, are more flexible and can be more objective) for a new approach to the problem.

Already we have begun to get responses from so-called Negro students from coast to coast, who aren't actually religiously inclined, but who are nonetheless strongly sympathetic to the approach used by Black Nationalism, whether it be social, economic, or political. And with this new approach and with these new ideas we think that we may open up a new era here in this country. As that era begins to spread, people in this country—instead of sticking under your nose or crying for civil rights—will begin to expand their civil rights plea to a plea for human rights. And once the so-called Negro in this country forgets the whole civil rights issue and begins to realize that human rights are far more important and broad than civil rights, he won't be going to Washington, D.C., anymore, to beg Uncle Sam for civil rights. He will take his plea for human rights to the United Nations. There won't be a violation of civil rights anymore. It will be a violation of human rights. Now at this moment, the governments that are in the United Nations can't step in, can't involve themselves with America's domestic policy. But the day the black man turns from civil rights to human rights, he will take his case into the halls of the United Nations in the same man-

ner as the people in Angola, whose human rights have been
violated by the Portuguese in South Africa.

You'll find that you are entering an era now where the
black man in this country has ceased to think domestically,
or within the bounds of the United States, and he's beginning to see that this is a world-wide issue and that he needs
help from outside. We need help from our brothers in
Africa who have won their independence. And when we
begin to show them our thinking has expanded to an international scale, they will step in and help us, and you'll find
that Uncle Sam will be in a most embarrassing position.
So the only way Uncle Sam can stop us is to get some civil
rights passed—right now! For if he can't take care of his
domestic dirt, it's going to be put before the eyes of the
world. Then you'll find that you'll have nobody on your
side, whatsoever, other than, perhaps, a few of those Uncle
Toms—and they've already out-lived their time. . . .

MODERATOR: I suggest we follow this format: We will have
reactions and responses to what Malcolm X has said from
the members of the panel, then give Malcolm X a chance
to discuss their views.

The first member of the panel to address us will be Professor James Q. Wilson, who has written an important book
about Negro politics in Chicago. At present, Professor
Wilson is Associate Professor of Government at Harvard
and also Director of the Joint Center for Urban Studies
[M.I.T. and Harvard].

JAMES Q. WILSON: Malcolm X, Ladies and Gentlemen. It is
impossible not to be impressed with the conviction, the
sincerity, the force and the vigor of the man who has
just spoken to you. He is protesting against outrages he
feels keenly. They are real outrages. They are outrages,
echoes of which can be found throughout American history, echoes raised by white and Negro voices alike.

The American political system, I suppose, is unique in many ways. One way it is unique is that it has a built-in resistance to fundamental, far-reaching change. This resistance to fundamental change has frustrated the efforts of people through two centuries of our history to achieve a fundamental social revolution short of force of arms. The system is, I believe, as Malcolm X has said, based on the *politics of hope*—hopes which politicians do not intend to realize. I think the reason is not because politicians are wicked men, and certainly not because they are more wicked than all of us, but because there is something inherent in the system which, on the one hand, induces them to offer promises and, on the other hand, prevents them from keeping them. We have had Populists, Socialists, Trotskyites, Greenbackers, and urban reformers, who for two centuries have railed against the system and this system has refused fundamentally to change—refused fundamentally to change for a variety of reasons. The chief reason, I suppose, is because politics in the long run has always paid off; that is, the politics of hope holds out to people in the long run the prospect, however dim and however uncertain, of freedom and of jobs and opportunity. And enough people have received these so that eventually their energies have been sapped and their enthusiasms converted.

The question, of course, is whether the politics of hope will work in this era when men such as Malcolm X are leading a new kind of social revolution in America. In the 1930's we used to say, with a note of relief in our voices, that there was no genuine Negro radical movement. There was no wholesale commitment of the Negroes to the Communist Party, because at that time there was no educated Negro middle class to provide the ideological cadres of such a revolutionary commitment. When the middle class was born, we pundits used to say, they would find the revolutionary consciousness in the event of a depression. Well, the revolutionary consciousness is now emerging, but not from the Negro middle class. The latter has been carried away with the politics of hope. I think Malcolm X would say it has been nicely "brought off" by the system. The revolutionary consciousness, we now find, is not a product of the middle class, but of the Negro lower class and of the young people, who have formed a kind of alliance unique in American politics, which proposes to change fundamentally the system in the direction of basic goals seen in visionary terms—which means they will be imperfectly realized.

A second question is how the American system will respond to this demand for fundamental change. The balance of power theory so long fashionable in discussions of the Negro vote is not true. The Negroes do not hold the balance of power in American politics for the same reason that no other single identifiable group holds the balance of power. And the reason that none of them do is that all of them do. The reason that all of them do is that American politics is so fragmented, so decentralized into bits and pieces of authority, so widely distributed over the constitutional landscape, that at any point in time almost any group can say with some plausibility that it contributed to the success of that politician. There is no national mandate. There is no national consensus. There is no politics in which one voice and one vote is the marginal voice, the marginal vote that decides the election.

The balance of power theory has been put to the test by third-party movements throughout our history, and the record has been a record of failure. No third party, with maybe one or two exceptions (which perhaps I tend to forget but conveniently ignore), has changed the outcome of any election in American history. No third party has ever become a major party. No third party, except for Teddy

Roosevelt's Bullmoosers, has ever become a second party. Only four ever received any electoral votes, and only three of these won as much as ten percent of the popular vote. To be sure, many of them were counted out by politicians when the ballot box was not so sacrosanct as it is today. Very few have ever won seats in Congress, and none have ever changed an election so far as we can be certain. One of the reasons why the balance of power theory has not contributed to the influence of third parties is because many groups within the two-party system can claim a whole share in this balance. It is true that in eight major northern industrial states, which together hold two hundred and ten electoral votes in the electoral college, the Negro vote for the Democratic candidate for President in 1960 was larger than the margin by which he defeated his Republican opponent in those states. Does this mean that the Negroes are responsible for his victory? It means they were only if you take into equal account that Catholics in those eight states also cast votes for the Democratic candidate in excess of plurality, that the Jews cast ballots in excess of plurality, young people and perhaps even college professors, God help us, cast ballots in excess of plurality. All these groups can say with equal plausibility that they hold the balance of power.

Gerrymandering is not the reason. There are many cities today in which Negroes are represented almost in proportion to their population. It is usually those cities which have shown the least progress in the direction of civil rights. Chicago has seven Negroes in the city council and nine Negroes in the state legislature. They are represented not precisely but nearly in accordance with their population. Yet Chicago and Illinois have been the slowest in taking any steps in the direction of major civil rights legislation. Negroes in New York are under-represented in politics. Yet this state has done far more for the Negro. Why? Because civil rights legislation by and large has not been aimed at capturing the Negro vote. The Negro vote could already be taken for granted by the Democratic Party. The civil rights legislation was therefore aimed at capturing the vote which was uncommitted, that independent vote which changes from election to election. And that was a vote of "supposedly liberal white friends" of the Negro, to use the former speaker's words.

It is fashionable today for Negroes to dislike and distrust their supposedly liberal white friends. It is just as fashionable for their supposedly liberal white friends to dislike and distrust themselves, for we are going through a period of anxiety in which we doubt our own capacity for action. We want something done collectively, but we cannot bring ourselves to act collectively. So we engage dubiously in personal relationships with students who need our help in Roxbury. The white liberal with his reticence, self-consciousness, and introspection today reflects precisely the same concern and the same charges the previous speaker has thrown at us. He does not need to indict us. We've indicted ourselves, and we know it. The question is where do we move in a system of this kind? John F. Kennedy did not ignore the promises he made to all the other groups that hold the balance of power. The trouble is that those promises canceled out each other. And this is not said in criticism of Kennedy. It is stated as characteristic of the system, and the question is how do you propose to change this? And is the change worthwhile? Perhaps it is; I don't know because I'm not a Negro, thank God. And perhaps from their point of view it is. I'm skeptical, but I remain open, I think, to persuasion. It is not deceitful Southern Democrats with civil rights filibustering who keep this legislation out of existence. The party label is about as meaningless as Malcolm X has so graphically pointed out.

Whether putting Negroes in office would change the *politics of hope* to the *politics of reality* is the real question. There are Negroes in office in almost every city and state of any consequence in the United States today. (I automatically exclude Mississippi.) What difference does this make? I don't know, but it's certainly not dramatic.

The white politicians cannot change the system. They've tried. I recall one time when there was a third party movement, an effort to capture certain key positions in the American political system and hold them long enough to force certain fundamental changes. In 1912 the Socialist Party in the United States captured six percent of the presidential vote. Almost nine hundred thousand people voted for its candidate for president. They elected fifty-six mayors, one hundred and sixty councilmen, one hundred and forty-five aldermen, eighteen state representatives, and two state senators. There were over one thousand Socialist Party members holding office in the United States at that time. They printed fourteen daily newspapers and two hundred ninety-eight weekly newspapers. They had one hundred eighteen thousand dues-paying members. And where is the Socialist Party today?

The Negro Party, if that is what is being proposed this evening, is not going to have precisely this outcome. Socialists can be lost in the American melting pot because the mark of their identity is carried inwardly and not outwardly. Negroes cannot be lost in this system because the mark of their identity is carried outward for all to see, for all time. The question is: Even though the spirit and the people and the movement continue to exist, what will happen if the strategy is a separatist strategy, a third-party strategy or even a strategy within a party to capture a party's leadership?

Is a separatist strategy going to accomplish as much as

those nonparty, and in some cases nonlegal, methods by
which the system is challenged directly by students sitting-
in, lying-in, kneeling-in, walking-in, or whatever? This
attacks the system in the one place where it is vulnerable
—its conscience, its slow, belated, fuzzy but existent conscience. When you start to play the political game, then
you're playing the game where the conscience is not involved for most people, because the political game is one
which people believe must be interpreted and explained
in cynical terms . . . cynical, because they know it hasn't
made any difference in the past; cynical, because they distrust the motives that go into politics and know that the
best things in life, from their point of view, come from
extra-political sources.

MODERATOR: The second speaker this evening will be Dr.
Martin L. Kilson. Dr. Kilson is Lecturer on Government
at Harvard, and will soon publish his first book, *Political
Change in a West African State.*

MARTIN KILSON: When I was working out my notes for this
evening, I thought that I would be the only one on this
panel who would end up being rather pessimistic and
somewhat cynical about things, because I am rather pessimistic about things, and what I have to say begins on a
pessimistic note and ends on a pessimistic note.

Now the first negative note that I want to begin on is
essentially about the way we modern Americans go about
political things in a modern social-cultural system. It seems
to me that the whole American political experiment and
experience and process always reflected what one would
call a certain kind of madness. By this I mean there has
always been a certain kind of emphasis upon the politically mundane and the politically vile as a means of staking
a claim for one's self or for one's group in the mainstream
of American society. Thus, for instance, the Irish, the Ital-
ians, and all of the other nineteenth century white immi-

grant groups fashioned quite consciously what, I think, can be called in a general way thoroughly corrupt, parochial political arrangements, in order to wrest out status and prestige and influence from the established patricians, Protestant elite groups; and through this to enter into the mainstream of American social life. We're told now that these white immigrants have quite succeeded. They have made it, so we are told; but unfortunately, the political arrangements they fashioned in order to succeed still persist at all levels of the American political system, and it is my feeling that they are about to strangle us all, including the sycamores on Memorial Drive. What is more, these mundane, corrupt, inefficient methods of allocating the resources of a modern society cannot really begin to handle the problem which the Negro confronts.

Then there came the Negro. Of course we came in the early 1900's from the South with great migration movements to the North and to the cities—what some thought to be the promised land. As former slaves, and therefore with immeasurably weaker positions in material and physical capacity for making way in an urban context, significantly few of these new Negroes could really fashion any meaningful stake in the mainstream of American society. But some, as the early middle-class Negroes, did attempt to fashion a stake in the mainstream, and, curiously enough, in close relationship with the corrupt political institutions created by the immigrant groups; who, indeed, tended to look upon the Negro as something less than a man. And so this peculiar kind of relationship between the early Negro middle class and national and state politicians appeared always to me a very curious kind of business. We're told too that this ten to fifteen or twenty percent of Negroes who have fashioned some kind of stake in American society have also "made it."

However, there remains the mass of Negroes who, it

seems, were in a small sense not so lucky. For even they, I think, still wanted to establish an estate in the American material heaven. And in a sense, why not? At their own level of cheap and exploited labor and human souls, they essentially contributed as much to the development of the American mainstream as any other group. In some respects, they contributed more than many groups. And this brings me to the question of the evening: the question of Black Nationalist politics and the conception of it which is now being propounded and organized by our speaker, Mr. Malcolm X.

Now it seems quite frankly that as another means of fashioning a foothold, a stake for the Negro in the American mainstream, the Black Nationalist, or any other black racist political proposition, is essentially as mundane and as vile as the institutions used successfully by the white immigrants. Yet, I think that the peculiar madness in American society has left the great mass of Negroes no really significant alternative method.

What is the method behind this kind of Black Nationalist proposition? I am myself totally willing to grant a good part of the description by Malcolm X and others of the position and experience of the Negro in American society. From such experiences has emerged a deep-seated frustration on the part of most Negroes as well as an ambivalent, love-hate complex, as it were, toward the white American majority. It is this frustration and complex upon which Malcolm X's Black Nationalist proposition must either stand or fall. Now, one can certainly query this business in more particular terms, and I do query it. But my thinking is that this is hardly a useful exercise, for as has been indicated, the Black Nationalist method is at its own level of experience, as "ethical" as techniques used by immigrant groups. In other words, self-styled maneuvering

is basically a legitimate part of this curious madness
I have in mind as being so characteristic of the American
political experiment. Therefore, it seems to me that
the really important question, at least from a social
scientist's point of view, is whether or not Mr.
Malcolm X's Black Nationalist proposition, or any other Black Nationalist proposition, can, in fact, make a greater claim for
the Negroes in the American mainstream. Now Mr. X
is necessarily optimistic on this point, or he wouldn't
be in business. But I myself am rather pessimistic on the
question. But I hasten to assure Mr. X that my pessimism
doesn't stem from any kind of unconscious wish that his
Black Nationalist method would fail. It rather stems from
my own reading of the complex and terrible plight that
most Negroes encounter today. And it also stems from my
reading of the past circumstances and forces that gave rise
to the first (at least organizationally successful) Black Nationalist proposition at the end of World War I (1918–
1925)—the Garvey Movement.

Now for one thing, I am convinced that among the sev-
enty-five percent of Negro Americans whom we can safely
call the Negro masses—that is, the poor and the downtrodden—there remains still some room for an effective Black
Nationalist political appeal. Indeed, the political history
of the urban Negro in this century, as I read it, reveals that
only the black racist appeal has ever been able to effectively
mobilize around political and social action any significant
portion of the Negro American population. This is precisely what Marcus Garvey and his *Universal Negro Improvement Association* demonstrated, even though at the
level of concrete contributions to the resolution of the
Negro problem it contributed, I think, essentially very
little. But today, in the middle of the twentieth century,
any Black Nationalist political group confronts the evident

fact that the circumstances which facilitated the Garvey movement have been significantly altered within the social structure of the urban Negro. Now I do not mean, of course, that the basic caste relationship of the Negro to the over-all white American society has been significantly altered. This relationship is basically the same as it has been for one century. What I do have in mind concerns the characteristics involved in the urban social structure of Negro society.

At the end of World War I it was interesting to note that urban Negro society was evolving basically along lines comparable to that of other groups. That is to say, it had an expanding structure of voluntary associations, which were slowly but surely meeting some of the basic day-to-day needs and problems of the urbanized mass. All the facts which I know reveal that the Garvey movement evolved within the framework of this expanding infrastructure of Negro voluntary associations, especially among the Negro masses. Even among the early small middle-class elements, some important middle-class personalities finally went over to the Garvey movement—people like Emmet J. Scott. Scott was an eminent Uncle Tom. He was a private secretary to Booker T. Washington, and upon Booker T. Washington's death inherited the whole structure of influence of that man; with that Scott became a partisan of the Garvey movement. But essentially, there were very few people this high up in the middle class who went over to the Garvey movement.

Today, however, you have a very different situation. With the exception of that twenty or twenty-five percent of middle-class Negroes who have some kind of stake in American society, who "have it made," for most Negroes this emergent and lively social structure of voluntary associations no longer prevails. The Great Depression dealt a

deadly blow to all spheres of the social structure of the
urban Negro masses. And today this structure stands in
essentially permanent disintegration. In fact, I wonder if
we cannot put it in the category of social pathology. But
not in the sense in which Mr. Epps was talking earlier. By
social pathology I mean something which is disintegrated
permanently, in a state of flux, incoherent, and all the rest.
. . . Data on all spheres of the poor urban Negro social
structure attest to this. Church attendance among poor
Negroes is essentially nonexistent. The family structure is so weak, so fluid, as to be meaningless; and the same
holds true for almost any index of effective meaningful
social structure among the seventy percent of poor urban
Negroes.

What is equally significant is the manner in which
the American system impinges upon this poor Negro social
structure; and how it has done nothing but intensify this
state of social pathology or of permanent social disintegration. For instance, all indices of social and economic well-
being find seventy percent of the Negro population at rock
bottom. Economic recessions of the forties, fifties, and of
the sixties have played havoc with this population, hitting
it at a rate normally two or three times that of the rest of
the population. In some urban centers in the past fifteen
years, where one finds a heavy Negro concentration, un-
employment has stood at twenty-five percent and more of
the adult male population. Thus, I myself cannot help
questioning whether a Black Nationalist proposition can
be successful in this state of tragic and terrible social disintegration. Frankly it is beyond comprehension that the
Nation of Islam, Mr. X's movement, or any other exclusively racist proposition could in and of itself even begin
to contribute a drop in the bucket. Nor do I think that the
politically mundane and the politically vile methods which

the white immigrants have bequeathed us can handle the job. In fact, I myself can see no basic, lasting, or meaningful resolution to the terrible plight of most Negroes within the present political arrangements and modes of thought that the American market place of political ideas has given us.

MODERATOR: Mr. X, I wonder if you'd like to reply to either Professor Wilson or Dr. Kilson.

MALCOLM X: As I said in my opening statement, I'm not a student of politics nor a politician, but I did learn a lot listening to the speakers. [Mr. Wilson] pointed out very decisively that politics won't solve the problem . . . this is what I got out of what he said . . . the politicians can't do it. In fact I can see now why the Honorable Elijah Muhammad said that complete separation is the only answer. For what I got from what he was saying is that Uncle Sam sees no hope within his political system of solving this problem that has become so complex that you can hardly even describe it. And this is why I said that we are issuing a call to youth, primarily, to get some new ideas and a new direction. The adults are more confused than the problem itself. It will take a whole generation of new people to approach this problem.

I would not like to leave the impression that I have ever, in any way, proposed a Negro party. Whoever entertains that thought is very much misinformed. We have never at any time advocated any kind of Negro party. The idea that I have been trying to convey is that Black Nationalism is our political philosophy. I didn't mention "party." By Black Nationalism I meant a political philosophy that makes the black man more conscious of the importance of his doing something to control his own destiny. The political philosophy maintained now by most black people in this country seems to me to leave their destiny in the hands of someone who doesn't even look like them. So, you see, the political philosophy of Black Nationalism has nothing to do with party. It is designed to make the black man develop some kind of consciousness or awareness of the importance of his shaping his own future, instead of leaving it to some segregationists in Washington, D.C., who come from the North as well as from the South. In pointing out that we are putting an accent on youth, we wish to let you know that our minds are wide open. We don't think we have the answer, but we are open-minded enough to try to seek the answer not from these old hicks, whom I think have gone astray, but from the youth. For the young may approach the problem from a new slant and perhaps come up with something that nobody else has thought of yet.

In reply to Dr. Kilson, who pointed out how Marcus Garvey failed: Marcus Garvey failed only because his movement was infiltrated by Uncle Toms, sent in by the government as well as by other bodies to maneuver him into a position wherein the government might have him sent to Atlanta, Georgia, put in a penitentiary, then deported, and his movement destroyed. But Marcus Garvey never failed. Marcus Garvey was the one who gave a sense of dignity to the black people in this country. He organized one of the largest mass movements that ever existed in this country; and his entire philosophy of organizing and attracting Negroes was based on going-back-to-Africa, which proves that the only mass movement which ever caught on in this country was designed to appeal to what the masses really felt. More of them then preferred to go back home than to stay here in this country and continue to beg the power structure for something they knew they would never get. Garvey did not fail. Indeed, it was Marcus Garvey's philosophy that inspired the Nkrumah fight for the independence of Ghana from the colonialism that was imposed on it by England. It is also the same Black Nationalism that has been spreading throughout Africa and that has brought about the emergence of the present independent African states. Garvey never failed. Garvey planted the seed which has popped up in Africa—everywhere you look! And although they're still trying to stamp it out in Angola, in South Africa, and in other places, you will soon be able to see for yourselves whether or not Garvey failed. He may have failed in America, but he didn't fail in Africa; and when Africa succeeds, you'll find that you have a new situation on your hands here in America.

I can't abide anyone referring to Black Nationalism as any kind of racism. Whenever white people get together they don't call it racism. The European Common Market is for Europeans; it excludes everyone else. In that case you don't call it racism; all the numerous blocks and groups and syndicates and cliques that the Western nations have formed are never referred to as racist. But when we dark people want to form some kind of united effort to solve our problem, either you or somebody you have brainwashed comes up with "racism." We don't call it racism; we call it brotherhood. To note just one more small point: it is true that a large middle-class group of so-called Negroes has developed in this country, and you may think that these Negroes are satisfied or that they want to stay here because they have a "stake." This is the popular misconception. The middle-class Negro in this country is almost more frustrated, disillusioned, and disenchanted than the Negro in the alley. Why? The Negro in the alley does not even think about integrating with you because he knows that he hasn't enough money to go where you are in control. So it doesn't enter his mind; he's less frustrated when he knows it's impossible. But this middle-class Negro, sharp as a tack with his Harvard accent and with his pocket full

of your money, thinks he should be able to go everywhere.
Indeed, he should be able to go everywhere, so he will try.

MODERATOR: I will take questions from the floor.

STUDENT QUESTION: I have a question for Mr. Malcolm X.
What is your view of the *Freedom Now Party*, which is certainly a third party movement? How do you feel about this
alternative way of solving the Negro problem?

MALCOLM X: I have met Negroes of the *Freedom Now
Party*, all of whom seem to be very militant. They are
young and militant and less likely to compromise. For these
reasons it offers more hope than other alternatives being
dangled in front of the so-called Negro. I couldn't say I
would endorse the *Freedom Now Party*, but my mind is
wide open to anything that will help gain progress.
In addition, members of the *Freedom Now Party* seem to
be more flexible than members of the Democratic and Republican parties. I don't think anything can be worse than
the Democrats and Republicans.

STUDENT QUESTION: Mr. Malcolm X, do you support a
bloody revolution and, if not, what kind do you have in
mind, especially when the Negro is at a numerical disadvantage?

MALCOLM X: Don't tell me about a six-to-one disadvantage. I agree it is a six-to-one disadvantage when you think
in terms of America. But in the world the nonwhite people
have you at an eleven-to-one disadvantage. We black
people consider ourselves a part of that vast body of dark
people who outnumber the whites, and we don't regard
ourselves as a minority.

STUDENT QUESTION: Mr. Malcolm X, you said the type of
civil rights agitation we see now has not altered the morality of white people. Could you comment on that?

MALCOLM X: When exposed to the methods of civil rights groups, whites remain complacent. You couldn't appeal to their ethical sense or their sense of legality. But, on the other hand, when they hear the analysis of the Honorable Elijah Muhammad, whites become more sharply attuned to the problem. They become more conscious of the problem. You can appeal to what intelligence whites have. Let the black man speak his mind so that the white man really knows how he feels. At the same time, let the white man speak his mind. Let everyone put his facts on the table. Once you put the facts on the table, it's possible to arrive at a solution.

The civil rights movement has put the white man in a position where he has to take a stand contrary to his intelligence. Many whites who do not support integration are afraid to say so when face to face with a Negro for fear the Negro will call him a bigot or a racist. So that even though a white in his intelligence can see that this forced integration will never work, he's afraid to say this to a black man; whereas if the white could speak his mind to the black man, he might wake that man up. My contention is that the approach used by the Honorable Elijah Muhammad is more realistic. A white man can speak his mind to a Muslim, and a Muslim is going to speak his mind to a white man. Once you establish this honest, sincere, realistic communication, you'll get a solution to the problem. But don't you give me that you love me and make me do the same thinking when there's nothing in our backgrounds nor anything around us which in any way gives either of us reason to love each other. Let's be real!

THE HARVARD LAW
SCHOOL FORUM OF
DECEMBER 16, 1964 [156]

Alan Dershowitz, Moderator

Our speaker this evening was born Malcolm Little about forty years ago in Omaha, Nebraska. Not much is known about his early life except that in 1948 he joined the Black Muslim Movement and adopted the last name of X, which he maintains today. Although still a Muslim, he has recently broken with the Black Muslim Movement, where he served as Chief Minister. He is now Chairman of an organization known as The Organization of Afro-American Unity —the description of which I shall leave to him. Now he prefers to be known as Brother Malcolm when he is speaking in a religious capacity, but as Malcolm X when he is speaking in a political capacity. *The New York Times* reported not very long ago that Malcolm X was the second most sought-after speaker on college and university campuses. The first was Barry Goldwater. Mr. Malcolm X.

Malcolm X

I first want to thank the Harvard Law School Forum for the invitation to speak here this evening, more especially to speak on a very timely topic—*The African Revolution and Its Impact on the American Negro*. I probably won't use the word "American Negro," but substitute "Afro-American." And when I say Afro-American, I mean it in the same context in which you usually use the word Negro. Our people today are increasingly shying away from use of that word. They find that when you're identified as Negro, it tends to make you "catch a whole lot of hell" that people who don't use it don't catch.

In the present debate over the Congo, you are probably aware that a new tone and a new tempo, almost a new temper, are being reflected among African statesmen toward the United States. And I think we should be interested in and concerned with what impact this will have upon Afro-Americans and how it will affect America's international race relations. We know that it will have an effect at the international level. It's already having such an effect. But I am primarily concerned with what effect it will have on the internal race relations of this country—that is to say, between the Afro-American and the white American.

When you let yourself be influenced by images created by others, you'll find that oftentimes the one who creates those images can use them to mislead you and misuse you. A good example: A couple of weeks ago I was on a plane with a couple of Americans, a male and a female sitting to my right. We were in the same row and had a nice conversation for about thirty-five to forty minutes. Finally the lady looked at my briefcase and said, "I would like to ask you a personal question," and I knew what was coming. She said, "What kind of last name could you have that begins with X?" I said, "Malcolm." Ten minutes went by, and she turned to me and said, "You're not Malcolm X?" You see, we had a nice conversation going, just three human beings, but she was soon looking at the image created by the press. She said so: "I just wouldn't believe that you were that man," she said.

I had a similar experience last week at Oxford. The Oxford Union had arranged a debate. Before the debate I had dinner with four students. A girl student looked kind of cross-eyed, goggle eyed and otherwise, and finally just told me she wanted to ask me a question. (I found out she was a conservative, by the way, whatever that is.) She said, "I just can't get over your not being as I had expected." I told her it was a case of the press carefully creating images.

Again I had a similar experience last night. At the United Nations a friend from Africa came in with a white woman who is involved with a philanthropic foundation over there. He and I were engaged in conversation for several minutes, and she was in and out of the conversation. Finally I heard her whisper to someone off to the side. She didn't think I was listening. She said—she actually said this—"He doesn't look so wild, you know." Now this is a full-grown, so-called "mature" woman. It shows the extent to which the press can create images. People looking for one thing actually miss the boat because they're looking for the wrong thing. They are looking for someone with horns, someone who is a rabble-rouser, an irrational, antisocial extremist. They expect to hear me say [that Negroes] should kill all the white people—as if you could kill all the white people! In fact, if I had believed what they said about the people in Britain, I never would have gone to Oxford. I would have let it slide. When I got there I didn't go by what I had read about them. I found out they were quite human and likable. Some weren't what I had expected.

Now I have taken time to discuss images because one of the sciences used and misused today is this science of [image making]. The power structure uses it at the local level, at the national level, at the international level. And oftentimes when you and I feel we've come to a conclusion on our own, the conclusion is something that someone has invented for us through the images he has created.

I'm a Muslim. Now if something is wrong with being

Muslim, we can argue, we can "get with it." I'm a Muslim, which means that I believe in the religion of Islam. I believe in Allah, the same God that many of you would probably believe in if you knew more about Him. I believe in all of the prophets: Abraham, Moses, Jesus, Muhammad. Most of you are Jewish, and you believe in Moses; you might not pick Jesus. If you're Christians, you believe in Moses and Jesus. Well, I'm Muslim, and I believe in Moses, Jesus, and Muhammad. I believe in all of them. So I think I'm "way up on you."

In Islam we practice prayer, charity, fasting. These should be practiced in all religions. The Muslim religion also requires one to make the pilgrimage to the Holy City of Mecca. I was fortunate enough to make it in April, and I went back again in September. Insofar as being a Muslim is concerned, I have done what one is supposed to do to be a Muslim.

Despite being a Muslim, I can't overlook the fact that I'm an Afro-American in a country which practices racism against black people. There is no religion under the sun that would make me forget the suffering that Negro people have undergone in this country. Negroes have suffered for no reason other than that their skins happen to be black. So whether I'm Muslim, Christian, Buddhist, Hindu, atheist or agnostic, I would still be in the front lines with Negro people fighting against the racism, segregation, and discrimination practiced in this country at all levels in the North, South, East, and West.

I believe in the brotherhood of all men, but I don't believe in wasting brotherhood on anyone who doesn't want to practice it with me. Brotherhood is a two-way street. I don't think brotherhood should be practiced with a man just because his skin is white. Brotherhood should hinge upon the deeds and attitudes of a man. I couldn't practice brotherhood, for example, with some of those Eastlands or crackers in the South who are responsible for the condition of our people.

I don't think anyone would deny either that if you send chickens out of your barnyard in the morning, at nightfall those chickens will come home to roost in *your* barnyard. Chickens that you send out always come back home. It is a law of nature. I was an old farm boy myself, and I got in trouble saying this once [about President Kennedy's assassination], but it didn't stop me from being a farm boy. Other people's chickens don't come to roost on your doorstep, and yours don't go to roost on theirs. The chickens that this country is responsible for sending out, whether the country likes it or not (and if you're mature, you look at it "like it is"), someday, and someday soon, have got to come back home to roost.

Victims of racism are created in the image of racists. When the victims struggle vigorously to protect themselves from violence of others, they are made to appear in the image of criminals; as the criminal image is projected onto the victim. The recent situation in the Congo is one of the best examples of this. The headlines were used to mislead the public, [to create] wrong images. In the Congo, planes were bombing Congolese villages, yet Americans read that (How do they say it?) American-trained anti-Castro Cuban pilots were bombing rebel strongholds. These pilots were actually dropping bombs on villages with women and children. But because the tags "American-trained" and "anti-Castro Cubans" were applied, the bombing was legal. Anyone against Castro is all right. The press gave them a "holier than thou" image. And you let them get away with it because of the labels. The victim is made the criminal. It is really mass murder—murder of women, children, and babies. And mass murder is disguised as a humanitarian project. They fool nobody but the people of America. They don't fool the people of the world, who see beyond the images.

Their man in the Congo is Tshombe, the murderer of the rightful Prime Minister of the Congo. No matter what kind of language you use, he's purely and simply a murderer. The real Prime Minister of the Congo was Patrice Lumumba. The American government—your and my government—took this murderer and hired him to run the Congo. He became their hired killer. And to show what a hired killer he is, his first act was to go to South Africa and to hire more killers, paying them with American dollars. But he is glorified because he is given the image of the only one who could bring stability to the Congo. Whether he can bring stability or not, he's still a murderer. The headlines spoke of white hostages, not simply hostages, but white hostages, and of white nuns and priests, not simply nuns and priests, but white nuns and priests. Why? To gain the sympathy of the white public of America. The press had to shake up your mind in order to get your sympathy and support for criminal actions. They tricked you. Americans consider forty white lives more valuable than four thousand black lives. Thousands of Congolese were losing their lives. Mercenaries were paid with American dollars. The American press made the murderers look like saints and the victims like criminals. They made criminals look like victims and indeed the devil look like an angel and angels like the devil.

A friend of mine from Africa, who is in a good position to know, said he believed the United States government is being advised by her worst enemy in the Congo, because an American citizen could not suggest such insane action—especially identifying with Tshombe, who is the worst African on earth. You cannot find an African on earth who is more hated than Tshombe. It's a justifiable hatred they have toward him. He has won no victory himself. His Congolese troops have never won a victory for him. Every victory has been won by white mercenaries, who are hired to kill for him. The African soldiers in the Congo are fighting for the Stanleyville government. Here Tshombe is a curse. He's an insult to anyone who means to do right, black or white. When Tshombe visited Cairo, he caused trouble. When he visited Rome last week, he caused trouble, and the same happened in Germany. Wherever Tshombe goes, trouble erupts. And if Tshombe comes to America, you'll see the worst rioting, bloodshed, and violence this country has ever seen. Nobody wants this kind of man in his country.

What effect does all this have on Afro-Americans? What effect will it have on race relations in this country? In the U.N. at this moment, Africans are using more uncompromising language and are heaping hot fire upon America as the racist and neo-colonial power par excellence. African statesmen have never used this language before. These statesmen are beginning to connect the criminal, racist acts practiced in the Congo with similar acts in Mississippi and Alabama. The Africans are pointing out that the white American government—not all white people—has shown just as much disregard for lives wrapped in black skin in the Congo as it shows for lives wrapped in black skin in Mississippi and in Alabama. When Africans, therefore, as well as we begin to think of Negro problems as interrelated, what will be the effect of such thinking on programs for improved race relations in this country? Many people will tell you that the black man in this country doesn't identify with Africa. Before 1959, many Negroes didn't. But before 1959, the image of Africa was created by an enemy of Africa, because Africans weren't in a position to create and project their own images. The image was created by the imperial powers of Europe.

Europeans created and popularized the image of Africa

as a jungle, a wild place where people were cannibals, naked and savage in a countryside overrun with dangerous animals. Such an image of the Africans was so hateful to Afro-Americans that they refused to identify with Africa. We did not realize that in hating Africa and the Africans we were hating ourselves. You cannot hate the roots of a tree and not hate the tree itself. Negroes certainly cannot at the same time hate Africa and love themselves. We Negroes hated the American features: the African nose, the shape of our lips, the color of our skin, the texture of our hair. We could only end up hating ourselves. Our skin became a trap, a prison; we felt inferior, inadequate, helpless. It was not an image created by Africans or by Afro-Americans, but by an enemy.

Since 1959 the image has changed. The African states have emerged and achieved independence. Black people in this country are crying out for their independence and show a desire to make a fighting stand for it. The attitude of the Afro-American cannot be disconnected from the attitude of the African. The pulse beat, the voice, the very life-drive that is reflected in the African is reflected today here among the Afro-Americans. The only way you can really understand the black man in America and the changes in his heart and mind is to fully understand the heart and mind of the black man on the African continent; because it is the same heart and the same mind, although separated by four hundred years and by the Atlantic Ocean. There are those who wouldn't like us to have the same heart and the same mind for fear that that heart and mind might get together. Because when our people in this country received a new image of Africa, they automatically united through the new image of themselves. Fear left them completely. There was fear, however, among the racist elements and the State Department. Their fear was of our sympathy for Africa and for its hopes and aspirations and of this sympathy developing into a form of alliance. It is only natural to expect us today to turn and look in the direction of our homeland and of our motherland and to wonder whether we can make any contact with her.

I grew up in Lansing, Michigan, a typical American city. In those days, a black man could have a job shining shoes or waiting tables. The best job was waiting tables at the country club, as is still the case in most cities. In those days, if a fellow worked at the State House shining shoes, he was considered a big shot in the town. Only when Hitler went on the rampage in 1939, and this country suffered a manpower shortage, did the black man get a shot at better jobs. He was permitted a step forward only when Uncle Sam had his back to the wall and needed him. In 1939, '40, and '41, a black man couldn't even join the Army or Navy, and when they began drafting, they weren't drafting black soldiers but only white. I think it was well agreed upon and understood: If you let the black man get in the Army, get hold of a gun, and learn to shoot it, you wouldn't have to tell him what the target was. It was not until the Negro leaders (and in this sense I use the word Negro purposely) began to cry out and complain—"If white boys are gonna die on the battlefields, our black boys must die on the battlefields too!"—that they started drafting us. If it hadn't been for that type of leadership, we never would have been drafted. The Negro leaders just wanted to show that we were good enough to die too, although we hadn't been good enough to join the Army or Navy prior to that time.

During the time that Hitler and Tojo were on the rampage, the black man was needed in the plants, and for the first time in the history of America, we were given an opportunity on a large scale to get skills in areas that were closed previously to us. When we got these skills, we were put in a position to get more money. We made more money. We moved to a better neighborhood. When we moved to a better neighborhood, we were able to go to a better school and to get a better education, and this put us into a position to know what we hadn't been receiving up to that time. Then we began to cry a little louder than we had ever cried before. But this advancement never was out of Uncle Sam's goodwill. We never made one step forward until world pressure put Uncle Sam on the spot. And it was when he was on the spot that he allowed us to take a couple of steps forward. It has never been out of any internal sense of morality or legality or humanism that we were allowed to advance. *You have been as cold as an icicle whenever it came to the rights of the black man in this country.* (Excuse me for raising my voice, but I think it's time. As long as my voice is the only thing I raise, I don't think you should become upset!)

Because we began to cry a little louder, a new strategy was used to handle us. The strategy evolved with the Supreme Court desegregation decision, which was written in such tricky language that every crook in the country could sidestep it. The Supreme Court desegregation decision was handed down over ten years ago. It has been implemented less than ten percent in those ten years. It was a token advancement, even as we've been the recipients of "tokenism" in education, housing, employment, everything. But nowhere in the country during the past ten years has the black man been treated as a human being in the same context as other human beings. He's always being patronized in a very paternalistic way, but never has he been given an opportunity to function as a human being. Actually, in one sense, it's our own fault, but I'll get to that later on. We have never gotten the real thing. (Heck, I'll get to it right now.) The reason we never received the real thing is that we have not displayed any tendency to do the same for ourselves which other human beings do: to protect our humanity and project our humanity.

I'll clarify what I mean. Not a single white person in America would sit idly by and let someone do to him what we black men have been letting others do to us. The white person would not remain passive, peaceful, and nonviolent. The day the black man in this country shows others that we are just as human as they in reaction to injustice, that we are willing to die just as quickly to protect our lives and property as whites have shown, only then will our people be recognized as human beings. It is inhuman, absolutely subhuman, for a man to let a dog bite him and not fight back. Let someone club him and let him not fight back, or let someone put water hoses on his women, his mother and daughter and babies and let him not fight back . . . then he's subhuman. The day he becomes a human being he will react as other human beings have reacted, and nobody [in humanity] will hold it against him.

In 1959, we saw the emergence of the Negro revolt and the collapse of European colonialism on the African continent. Our struggle, our initiative, and our militancy were in tune with the struggle and initiative and militancy of our brothers in Africa. When the colonial powers saw they couldn't remain in Africa, they behaved as somebody playing basketball. He gets the basketball and must pass it to a teammate in the clear. The colonial powers were boxed in on the African continent. They didn't intend to give up the ball. They just passed it to the one that was in the clear, and the one that was in the clear was the United States. The ball was passed to her, and she picked it up and has been running like mad ever since. Her presence on the African continent has replaced the imperialism and the colonialism of Europeans. But it's still imperialism and colonialism. Americans fooled many of the Africans into thinking that they weren't an imperialist power or colonial power until their intentions were revealed, until they hired Tshombe and put him back to kill in the Congo. Nothing America could have done would have ever awakened the Africans to her true intentions as did her dealings with this murderer named Tshombe.

America knew that Africa was waking in '59. Africa was developing a higher degree of intelligence than she reflected in the past. America, for her part, knew she had to use a more intelligent approach. She used the friendly approach: the Peace Corps, Crossroads. Such philanthropic acts disguised American imperialism and colonialism with dollar-ism. America was not honest with what she was doing. I don't mean that those in the Peace Corps weren't honest. But the Corps was being used more for political purposes than for moral purposes. I met many white Peace Corps workers while on the African continent. Many of them were properly motivated and were making a great contribution. But the Peace Corps will never work over there until the idea has been applied over here.

Of course the Civil Rights Bill was designed supposedly to solve our problem. As soon as it was passed, however, three civil rights workers were murdered. Nothing has been done about it, and I think nothing will be done about it until the people themselves do something about it. I, for one, think the best way to stop the Ku Klux Klan is to talk to the Ku Klux Klan in the only language it understands, for you can't talk French to someone who speaks German and communicate. Find out what language a person speaks, speak their language, and you'll get your point across. Racists know only one language, and it is doing the black man in this country an injustice to expect him to talk the language of peace to people who don't know peaceful language. In order to get any kind of point across our people must speak whatever language the racist speaks. The government can't protect us. The government has not protected us. It is time for us to do whatever is necessary by any means necessary to protect ourselves. If the government doesn't want us running around here wild like that, then I say let the government get up off its . . . whatever it's on, and take care of it itself. After the passage of the Civil Rights Bill, they killed the Negro educator Pitt in Georgia. The killers were brought to court and then set free. This is the pattern in this country, and I think that white people (I use the word white people because it's cut short; it gets right to the point) are doing us an injustice. If you expect us to be nonviolent, you yourselves aren't. If someone came knocking on your door with a rifle, you'd walk out of the door with your rifle. Now the black man in this country is getting ready to do the same thing.

I say in conclusion that the Negro problem has ceased to be a Negro problem. It has ceased to be an American problem and has now become a world problem, a problem for all humanity. Negroes waste their time confining their struggle to civil rights. In that context the problem remains only within the jurisdiction of the United States. No allies can help Negroes without violating United States protocol. But today the black man in America has seen his mistake and is correcting it by lifting his struggle from the level of civil rights to the level of human rights. No longer does the United States government sit in an ivory tower where it can point at South Africa, point at the Portuguese, British, French, and other European colonial powers. No longer can the United States hold twenty million black people in second-class citizenship and think that the world will keep a silent mouth. No matter what the independent African states are doing in the United Nations, it is only a flicker, a glimpse, a ripple of what this country is in for in the future, unless a halt is brought to the illegal injustices which our people continue to suffer every day.

The Organization of Afro-American Unity (to which I belong) is a peaceful organization based on brotherhood. Oh yes, it is peaceful. But I believe you can't have peace until you're ready to protect it. As you will die protecting yours, I will die protecting mine. The OAAU is trying to get our problem before the United Nations. This is one of its immediate projects on the domestic front. We will work with all existing civil rights organizations. Since there has been talk of minimizing demonstrations and of becoming involved in political action, we want to see if civil rights organizations mean it. The OAAU will become involved in every move to secure maximum opportunity for black people to register peacefully as voters. We believe that along with voter registration, Afro-Americans need voter education. Our people should receive education in the science of politics so that the crooked politician cannot exploit us. We must put ourselves in a position to become active politically. We believe that the OAAU should provide defense units in every area of this country where workers are registering or are seeking voting rights, in every area where young students go out on the battlefront (which it actually is). Such self-defense units should have brothers who will not go out and initiate aggression, but brothers who are qualified, equipped to retaliate when anyone imposes brutally on us, whether it be in Mississippi, Massachusetts, California, or New York City. The OAAU doesn't believe it should permit civil rights workers to be murdered. When a government can't protect civil rights workers, we believe we should do it. Even in the Christian Bible it says that he who kills with the sword shall be killed by

the sword, and I'm not against it. I'm for peace, yet I believe that any man facing death should be able to go to any
length to assure that whoever is trying to kill him doesn't
have a chance. The OAAU supports the plan of every civil
rights group for political action, as long as it doesn't involve
compromise. We don't believe Afro-Americans should be
victims any longer. We believe we should let the world
know, the Ku Klux Klan know, that bloodshed is a two-
way street, that dying is a two-way street, that killing is a
two-way street. Now I say all this in as peaceful a language
as I know.

There was another man back in history whom I read
about once, an old friend of mine whose name was Hamlet,
who confronted, in a sense, the same thing our people are
confronting here in America. Hamlet was debating whether
"To be or not to be"—that was the question. He was trying to decide whether it was "nobler in the mind to suffer
(peacefully) the slings and arrows of outrageous fortune,"
or whether it was nobler "to take up arms" and oppose
them. I think his little soliloquy answers itself. As long as
you sit around suffering the slings and arrows and are afraid
to use some slings and arrows yourself, you'll continue to
suffer. The OAAU has come to the conclusion that it is
time to take up whatever means necessary to bring these
sufferings to a halt.

MODERATOR: Our next speaker is Mr. Archie Epps; Mr.
Epps has been active in civil rights work in the Boston area.

ARCHIE EPPS: I am told that Negro boys have invented a
little game they play in the streets of Harlem, New York.
One boy will stand at one end of the street and yell Lumumba. Another boy at the other end of the street will yell
Kasavubu. Both will then rush toward each other, impro-
vising an African dance. A mock duel will then be fought,
expressing both their pride at playing the role of African

heroes and their awareness of a conflict between rival political leaders on another continent. At this level of awareness, Africa has surely had an impact on American Negroes.

The successful evolution of African independent states, however, bears only indirectly on the American Negro revolution. A racial theory of revolution has been used by Malcolm X this evening to describe the Negro revolutions in Africa and America. On one side, he drew an analogy between European colonization and American slavery and segregation. It was argued that since the white man established these systems of exploitation, he was the common enemy of the American Negro and the Africans. The accuracy of this theory of revolution is questionable, especially since it assumes that a worldwide conspiracy of white men will be overthrown by a conspiracy of black man. This conspiracy theory perpetuates false images. One such image is the ostensible desire by Negro leaders to free their people in America and Africa.

Furthermore, this argument takes one away from historical reality. Negroes have (and have had) a hand in the oppression of their own people. Explanation of the slave trade by a white conspiracy theory is, therefore, full of hypocrisy and provides an insufficient premise for the justification of self-righteous Negro revolutions.

A major obstruction to Negro advancement in America is this ostensible radicalism of Negro leaders which really masks a political conservatism. These Negro leaders live by an essentially undemocratic notion of their role. They believe that Negro communities should delegate all decision-making to them. The most conservative imply that the Negro masses are culturally inferior and politically inept. Where a religious elite holds sway, as in the Black Muslim Movement, the masses are thought to be in need of total moral reconstruction. Negro elite of this sort have perpetu-

ated (and perpetuate) an authoritarian and explicitly undemocratic tradition of political rule in the whole array of
American Negro religious and political organizations. By
and large, this single ideological tradition has left Negro
groups, middle class and otherwise, to fend for themselves
in the modern world without progressive political institutions.

Actually, these elite leaders use an ideology of common
racial origin to perpetuate themselves in office. Accordingly, Negroes should not criticize one another since "blood
brothers" should stick together at all costs. I have time only
to deal with one American example of this. At the Democratic National Convention of 1964, Negro Democrats
failed to help the Mississippi Freedom Democratic Party
to gain recognition. One hundred twenty-six official Negro
delegates of the convention decided in caucus not to give
public support to that party. The predominantly Negro
MFDP had claimed that it was the rightful representative
of Mississippi Democrats. It had asked the Convention to
seat its delegates instead of the regular all-white Democratic Party delegates. The MFDP charged that Negroes
had been systematically excluded from Democratic Party
meetings in Mississippi. It accused the regular Democratic
Party of Mississippi of full-fledged discrimination. The
MFDP claimed, furthermore, that less than seven percent
of eligible Negroes in the state were registered to vote because of a combination of poll tax assessment, harassment,
and discriminatory voting tests. Confronted with tales of
Negro persecution, with which they were surely familiar,
a large majority of the one hundred twenty-six Negro delegates turned a deaf ear to the MFDP.

However, these Negro leaders were not through. Another caucus was held an hour later at which it was ru-
mored that a Negro Congressman would take up the prob-

lem of the MFDP. MFDP supporters thought that the
Congressman would surely throw his support their way
and criticize Negro delegation inaction and lack of courage.
He was, after all, the leader of a predominantly Negro
political machine. Instead, the Negro leader elaborated a
theory of the need for total delegation of decision on the
MFDP question to him. He argued that the MFDP Convention challenge was a repudiation of his mandate as chief
political leader of the Negro delegates. He lectured the
group on the need for proper respect of his authority. He
said that as a Negro and as a Democrat he could promise
that something would be done about the exclusion of
Negro Democrats from party membership in Mississippi,
but at some other time. He continually repeated, "*We* are
your leaders." The MFDP delegates and civil rights workers went away disappointed, abandoning their appeal to
Negro leaders. They chose instead a strategy of protest.
The following evening, MFDP delegates executed a "sit-
in" at the Convention in seats reserved for the white
Mississippi delegation.

Negro conservatism in America takes forms besides the
explicitly political. Negro prophet churches and sects propose other-worldly solutions to what are really political
problems. Daddy Grace and Prophet Jones have thrown up
separatist religio-political organizations which siphon off
the already meager financial resources of poor Negroes.
These prophet movements dispense Puritan righteousness
to the Negro proletariat, each generation of Negroes seeing
these prophetic movements as solutions to problems of poverty and segregation. In fact, Malcolm X has emerged out
of this same cycle of hope and disappointment. Negro religious conservatism actually works hand-in-hand with political conservatism to maintain the status quo, rendering the
energy of the Negro masses irrelevant to the modernization

of the Negro minority. The relevant issue for debate here then is the nature of the political reality with which a Negro leader must deal.

Social reform of the sort we are discussing is very seldom initiated by an elite. It will surely not be initiated by incumbent Negro political leaders. Actually, the Negro masses of Africa and America will likely express themselves in a crazy-quilt pattern of political assertion. They will believe they are helping to win a "place in the sun" by threatening the rich. Those who would be leaders of masses, therefore, had best figure out what form this mass political expression will take and try to render it more rational. Malcolm X's immediate problem, then, is to see why other leaders of his type have failed and try to avoid their mistakes. The Garvey Movement failed because of its great emphasis on a glorious Africa, which, in reality, was only a dream in Garvey's head. Garvey had the Negro masses searching for the end of a rainbow, while he huffed and puffed about what he could do to the white man if given the chance. The poor Negro folk of the South and North contributed two million dollars to his United Negro Improvement Association to give him that chance. He did nothing for them but continue to talk of his dream of uniting black men around the world. Malcolm X's hands-across-the-water strategy with Africa seems to be based on the same irrelevant dream.

American Negro cooperation with Africa will come about someday. Hopefully the purpose of this cooperation will be not to fashion a black chauvinistic alliance in order to contend for world-wide power, but to advance civility and humane government, to remove violence and hatred from the political relationships of nations and races.

I was disappointed to hear Malcolm X refer again, without real qualification and rather gleefully, to the Kennedy assassination as "chickens coming home to roost." I assume that Malcolm X uses the saying to explain the violent tradition in American history, which he would describe as the inevitable drift of history toward retribution. I believe, on the contrary, that men are not the servants of history, whatever the tradition, but at least aspiring free agents. The Negro is not a member of the race of Sisyphus—required by divine decree to push a rock up a mountain only to have it roll down again. Malcolm X's view of history is inherently pessimistic. This view does not allow that Negroes are no longer slaves, but are, in part, free agents. Negro efforts at reform in America, and in Africa, for that matter, must seek an honest appraisal of what use Negroes have made of the opportunities to lead. Where these opportunities were misused, based on archaic political philosophies, or were inhumane, then the Negro must bear a portion of the responsibility for his oppression.

The real work of the day for the Negro American, as Malcolm X's honesty has helped us begin to realize, is to confront the hypocrisy of both white and Negro institutions, to criticize undemocratic policies wherever they are found, and to oppose the injustice of discrimination and segregation.

Malcolm X's Hamlet was more correctly represented by the Negro boys playing that same game in the Harlem street, dancing to the names of Lumumba and Kasavubu, already aware of human folly. They were caught at the crosscurrent of children's play and an adult world. Malcolm X oversimplified Hamlet's soliloquy to threaten whites with violence. To me, Hamlet's soliloquy represents man at the height of indecision, of his confusion over the contemplation of hatred and love. Hamlet was no model of violent political action. He was rather a model of the human condition, of man trapped between the wretchedness of life and belief in human goodness.

MODERATOR: The floor will be open for questions.

STUDENT QUESTION: Mr. X, do you feel that the awarding of the Nobel Peace Prize to Dr. Martin Luther King has in any way helped the Negro cause in the United States?

MALCOLM X: Black people in this country have no peace and have not made the strides forward that would in any way justify receiving a reward by any of us. The war is not won nor has any battle been won. But I have no comment to make about my good friend, Dr. King.

STUDENT QUESTION: Sir, I would like to know the difference between a white racist and a black racist, besides the fact that they are white and black.

MALCOLM X: Usually the black racist has been produced by the white racist. And in most cases, black racism is in reaction to white racism. If you analyze it very closely, you will find that it is not black racism. Black people have shown fewer tendencies toward racism than any people since the beginning of history. I cannot agree with my brother here who says that Negroes are immoral; that's what I get out of what he said. It is the whites who have committed violence against us.

STUDENT QUESTION: I am one of the whites who agrees with you one hundred percent. You pointed out that the majority of Negro people voted for Johnson, and then he invaded the Congo, something which Goldwater did not even advocate. What do you propose that black people should do in future elections?

MALCOLM X: First our people should become registered voters. But they should not become actively involved in politics until we have also gotten a much better understanding of the game of politics in this country. We go into politics in a sort of gullible way, where politics in this country is cold-blooded and heartless. We need a better understanding of the science of politics as well as becoming registered voters. And then we should not take sides either way. We should reserve political action for the situation at hand, in no way identifying with either political party (the Democrats or the Republicans) or selling ourselves to either party. We should take political action for the good of human beings; that will eliminate the injustices.

I for one do not think that the man presently in the White House is morally capable of taking the kind of action necessary to eliminate these things.

STUDENT QUESTION: Mr. X, your idea of an Afro-American is a very hard lump to swallow. James Baldwin, in describing a conference of African writers and politicians which took place in Paris in 1956, reported that the conference had difficulty in defining an African personality common to all countries in Africa and to the American Negroes. The members of the conference, including James Baldwin, began to realize that there was a big rift between American Negroes and the people from Africa. The American Negro has a totally different set of values and ideas from that of the African. Therefore, if you still talk about the Afro-American in which the only connection is the color of the skin, this is a racist concept. Why emphasize Afro-American, which is a racist concept and a reactionary concept, instead of something more positive?

MALCOLM X: I do not think that anything is more positive than accepting what you are. The Negro in America tries to be more American than anyone else. The [attempt] has created a person who is actually negative in almost everything he reflects. We are just as much African today as we were in Africa four hundred years ago, only we are a modern counterpart of it. When you hear a black man playing music, whether it is jazz or Bach, you still hear African music. The soul of Africa is still reflected in the music played by black men. In everything else we do we still are African in color, feeling, everything. And we will always be that whether we like it or not.

FOOTNOTES

Part One / The Paradoxes of Malcolm X

3. Karl Marx, *The Eighteenth Brumaire of Louis Bonaparte* (New York, based on the Hamburg Edition of 1869, 1963), p. 20.
4. Malcolm X, *The Autobiography*, p. 387.
5. The tertiary elite, a new concept suggested by my colleague Martin Kilson, is at once a descriptive and conceptual idea used to isolate that leadership stratum which is nearest the Negro lower class. Above the tertiary elite is the Negro middle class and below, in considerable disarray, is the Negro lower class. Tertiary elite are owners of barbershops, flop houses, store-front church clergy, etc. This group mans the very practically oriented institutions whose stability over the years is a hallmark of this elite's ability to make do in the modern world on very limited resources.
6. A. Jacques Garvey, *Garvey and Garveyism* (Jamaica, 1963), p. 134.
7. Malcolm X, *The Autobiography*, pp. 4–10.   8. *Ibid.*, p. 37.
9. Karl Marx, *The Eighteenth Brumaire*, p. 20.
10. Malcolm X, *The Autobiography*, p. 37.   11. *Ibid.*, p. 63.
12. *Ibid.*, p. 34.   13. *Ibid.*, p. 34.   14. *Ibid.*, p. 60.
15. *Ibid.*, p. 110.   16. *Ibid.*, p. 87.   17. *Ibid.*, p. 131.
18. *Ibid.*, p. 131.

19. Lady Day, "You Don't Know What Love Is," composed by Don Raye and Gene de Paul (New York, 1941).

20. Lawrence O'Kane, "Muslim Negroes Suing the State," *New York Times* (March 19, 1961), pp. 1, 46.

21. Arna Bontemps and Jack Conroy, *Anyplace But Here* (New York, 1966), pp. 225–226.

22. Account of radio broadcasts was made in the newspaper, *Muhammad Speaks,* Spring issue, 1962.

23. E. U. Essien-Udom, *Black Nationalism* (Chicago, 1962), p. 172.

24. Louis E. Lomax, *When The Word Is Given* (Cleveland, 1963), pp. 209–210.

25. George Breitman, ed., *Malcolm X Speaks* (New York, 1965), pp. 18–22.   26. *Ibid.*, pp. 21–22.

27. E. Franklin Frazier, *The Negro Church In America* (New York, 1963), pp. 55, 65.

28. Malcolm X, *The Harvard Law School Forum of March 24, 1961.*

29. Malcolm X, *The Harvard Law School Forum of December 16, 1964.*

30. Malcolm X, *The Leverett House Forum of March 18, 1964.*

31. Malcolm X, *The Harvard Forum of December 16, 1964.*

32. Theodore Jones, "Malcolm Knew He Was A 'Marked Man,'" *The New York Times* (February 22, 1965), pp. 6, 10.

33. Doris Lessing, "Allah Be Praised," *New Statesman* (May 27, 1966), pp. 775–778.

34. Malcolm X, *The Harvard Forum of December 16, 1964.*

35. Karl Marx, *The Eighteenth Brumaire,* p. 44.

36. Theodore Jones, *op. cit.,* p. 10.

37. "Malcolm X Guard Explains Inaction," *The New York Times* (January 27, 1966), p. 6.

38. Jan Kott, *Shakespeare Our Contemporary* (Anchor Books Edition, 1966), p. 37.

39. Malcolm X, *The Harvard Forum of December 16, 1964.*

40. Jan Kott, *op. cit.,* p. 33.

41. *Ibid.,* p. 30.

42. Malcolm X, *The Autobiography,* p. 384.

43. Jan Kott, *Shakespeare Our Contemporary,* p. 31.

44. Ralph Ellison, *Shadow And Act* (New York, 1964), p. 131.

45. George Breitman, ed., *Malcolm X Speaks,* p. 13.

46. *Ibid.,* p. 229.   47. *Ibid.,* p. 215.   48. *Ibid.,* pp. 143–144.

49. Malcolm X, *The Autobiography,* p. 251.

50. *Ibid.,* p. 35.   51. *Ibid.,* p. 10.   52. *Ibid.,* p. 387.
53. Denis Donoghue, *The New York Review of Books* (August, 1966), p. 8.
54. A. Jacques Garvey, *Garvey and Garveyism,* p. 23.
55. Paul Oliver, *The Meaning of the Blues* (New York, 1960), p. 141.
56. Kenneth Burke, *Attitudes Toward History* (Boston, Beacon Edition, 1961), p. 4.
57. Elijah Muhammad, *Message To The Blackman In America* (Chicago, 1965).   58. *Ibid.,* p. 292.
59. Malcolm X, *The Autobiography,* p. 309.
60. *Ibid.,* pp. 187–188.   61. *Ibid.,* p. 189.
62. *Ibid.,* pp. 189–190.   63. *Ibid.,* p. 190.   64. *Ibid.,* p. 190.
65. Paul Oliver, *The Meaning of the Blues,* p. 307. The quotation is taken from a blues song sung by Red Nelson in 1935. Nelson sang:

> Black cat calls me out at midnight,
> Nightmares ride to the break of dawn
>   (Twice)
> What's the use of loving some woman,
> Some man done stole your love away.
> I used to have a sweet woman to love me,
> Now she treats me like a low-down dog.

66. *Ibid.,* pp. 335, 301. The first line was taken from the "Milk Cow Blues" by Nokomo Arnold, 1935. The second line was from the "Hooting Owl Blues" by Dolly Ross, 1927.
67. *Ibid.,* p. 287. The lines were from the "Training Camp Blues" by Roosevelt Sykes, 1941.
68. Malcolm X, *The Autobiography,* p. 35.
69. Lewis Allan, "Strange Fruit," adapted to music by Billie Holiday. Cf. *The Best of Billie Holiday* (New York, 1962), pp. 11–13.
70. George Breitman, ed., *Malcolm X Speaks,* pp. 142–143. Also, Robert Penn Warren, *Who Speaks For The Negro* (New York, 1965), p. 261.
71. Louis Lomax, *When The Word Is Given,* p. 67.
72. Lady Day, *op. cit.,* pp. 11–13.
73. George Breitman, ed., *Malcolm X Speaks,* p. 22.
74. *Ibid.,* p. 130.   75. *Ibid.,* pp. 4, 13.
76. Malcolm X, *The Harvard Forum of December 16, 1964.*

77. Malcolm X, *The Harvard Forum of March 24, 1961.*
78. John Illo, "The Rhetoric of Malcolm X," *Columbia University Forum* (Spring, 1966), p. 9.
79. *Ibid.,* p. 9. Mr. Illo quotes Malcolm X here without citation.
80. *Ibid.,* p. 9. Malcolm X used the same imagery in the Audubon Speech of January 24, 1965; cf. "Malcolm X on Afro-American History," *International Socialist Review* (March–April, 1967), p. 15.   81. *Ibid.,* p. 9.
82. *Ibid.,* p. 9.   83. *Ibid.,* p. 9.   84. *Ibid.,* pp. 9, 10.
85. *Ibid.,* p. 10.   86. *Ibid.,* p. 10.   87. *Ibid.,* pp. 10–11.
88. Malcolm X, *The Harvard Forum of December 16, 1964.* Malcolm X used an almost identical formulation of this interdependence of the American Negroes on the image of Africa in a speech in Detroit, Michigan, on February 13, 1965. See Breitman, ed., *Malcolm X Speaks,* p. 184. He had obviously memorized paragraphs to use in speeches during this period or spoke from an outline which contained fully written-out sections.
89. George Breitman, ed., *Malcolm X Speaks,* p. 130.
90. John Illo, "The Rhetoric of Malcolm X," p. 6.
91. *Ibid.,* p. 5.
92. *The New Republic* (August 13, 1966), p. 11. This statement was attributed to John Hubett of the Black Panther Party of Alabama.
93. "Crises of Color '66," *Newsweek* (August 22, 1966), p. 27.
94. Elijah Muhammad, *Message To The Blackman,* p. 33.
95. Louis Lomax, *When The Word Is Given,* p. 162.
96. *Ibid.,* p. 163.
97. Johnie Scot, "My Home Is Watts," *Harper's* (October, 1966), p. 48.
98. George Breitman, ed., *Malcolm X Speaks,* pp. 11–12.
99. *Ibid.,* p. 12.   100. *Ibid.,* pp. 7, 9, 10.
101. *Ibid.,* pp. 13, 14. The order of Malcolm X's paragraphs has been changed for emphasis. For correct order, see Breitman, *Malcolm X Speaks,* as cited.
102. *Ibid.,* p. 14.   103. *Ibid.,* p. 13.
104. Malcolm X, "Message To The Grass Roots," *Afro-American Broadcasting and Recording Company,* Record Jacket (Detroit, 1965), Sides 1 and 2.
105. Countee Cullen, *Black Christ and Other Poems* (London, 1929), pp. 66–91.
106. A. Jacques Garvey, *Garvey and Garveyism,* pp. 22, 24.

107. E. U. Essien-Udom, *Black Nationalism*, pp. 103–104.
108. Louis Lomax, *When The Word Is Given*, p. 85.
109. Malcolm X, *The Harvard Forum of December 16, 1964.*
110. John Illo, "The Rhetoric of Malcolm X," p. 10.
111. Malcolm X, *The Harvard Forum of December 16, 1964.*
112. Jan Kott, *Shakespeare Our Contemporary*, p. 40.
113. *Ibid.*, p. 40.
114. George Breitman, ed., *Malcolm X Speaks*, p. 4.
115. Ralph Ellison, "Harlem's America," *The New Leader* (September, 1966), p. 24.
116. Ralph Ellison, *Shadow And Act*, p. 254.
117. Malcolm X, "Afro-American History," p. 16.
118. *Ibid.*, p. 17.
119. Malcolm X, *The Harvard Forum of March 24, 1961.*
120. Jan Kott, *Shakespeare Our Contemporary*, p. 82.
121. *Ibid.*, p. 141.
122. Malcolm X, *The Harvard Forum of March 24, 1961.*
123. Jan Kott, *Shakespeare Our Contemporary*, p. 142.
124. *Ibid.*, p. 143.
125. Ronald Sullivan, "Racism Linked To 'Spineless Leaders.'" Statement attributed to Mayor Thomas J. Whelan of Jersey City, New Jersey. A speech before the 71st Annual Convention of the New Jersey Patrolmen's Benevolent Association. Cf. text of speech, p. 7. The quotation is completed thus: ". . . The degenerate thugs who hide in darkened windows and shoot down police and firemen will be rewarded and encouraged to shoot and loot again." *The New York Times* (Early City Edition, September 27, 1967). Mr. Sullivan was kind enough to discuss this speech with me.
126. John P. Corr, "D'Ortona Urges Hiring of 1000 New Policemen." City Council President Paul D'Ortona commenting on the North Philadelphia Riot of August 28, 29, 1967. *The Philadelphia Inquirer* (September 1, 1964), p. 1, 3.
127. Jan Kott, *Shakespeare Our Contemporary*, p. 146.
128. Samuel Beckett, "Act Without Words I," *Krapp's Last Tape and Other Dramatic Pieces* (First European Edition, 1960), p. 132.
129. Malcolm X, *The Harvard Forum of March 24, 1961.*
130. *Ibid.*
131. Jan Kott, *Shakespeare Our Contemporary*, p. 114.
132. Anna Bontemps and Jack Conroy, *Anyplace But Here* (New York, 1966), p. 242.

133. Malcolm X, *The Harvard Forum of March 18, 1964*.
134. *Ibid.*   135. *Ibid.*   136. *Ibid.*   137. *Ibid.*
138. *Ibid.*
139. Martin Kilson, "On Black Power," unpublished essay (Fall, 1967), p. 8.
140. *Ibid.*, p. 9.
141. Jan Kott, *Shakespeare Our Contemporary*, p. 77.
142. *Ibid.*, p. 77.
143. Malcolm X, *The Harvard Forum of December 16, 1964*.
144. *Ibid.*
145. Jan Kott, *Shakespeare Our Contemporary*, p. 62.
146. *Ibid.*, p. 62.   147. *Ibid.*, p. 69.
148. Malcolm X, *The Harvard Forum of December 16, 1964*.
149. Malcolm X, "Afro-American History," p. 33.
150. Malcolm X, *The Autobiography*, p. 309.
151. George Breitman, ed., *Malcolm X Speaks*, p. 116.
152. Robert Penn Warren, "Malcolm X: Mission and Meaning," *The Yale Review*, Vol. LVI, No. 2, pp. 161–162.
153. Jan Kott, *Shakespeare Our Contemporary*, p. 57. The poem quoted here is used just as it appears in Kott, without punctuation. The translation is by Creslaw Milosz.

Part Two / The Harvard Speeches

154. This speech was published in Louis Lomax's *When The Word Is Given*, 1963. I have simply reorganized the paragraphs of this speech around seven sub-subjects which strike the eye right off. The reader will find that Malcolm X discussed the following: (a) the doctrines of the Nation of Islam; (b) the message of the Nation of Islam; (c) the old world and the new world; (d) the black masses; (e) orthodox Islam and the Nation of Islam; (f) integration and separation; (g) the judgment of Allah.

 Although I have not documented this, this speech seemed to use Elijah Muhammad's language. In particular we have a rare example of something which was probably characteristic of the early phase of the movement, namely, the creation of words. Malcolm X used the word "missioned," which I have rendered "commissioned." This speech was delivered from a prepared text, but Mr. Lomax's editing indicates that much has been left out.

155. The Leverett House Forum was an interesting event. Most of Malcom X's performances on public platforms with opponents had seemed to me, at least, sort of public rituals: Malcolm X would give the Black Muslim line and the opponent would disclaim any interest whatsoever in the weight of the Malcolm X position and would certainly not consider it an alternate popular Negro strategy. It was my duty as moderator of the Leverett Forum to try and arrange a more honest and hopefully productive public meeting. My colleagues, Martin Kilson and James Q. Wilson, were most cooperative in this regard. They agreed to participate in the Forum. And, what was most important, I knew they took the subject of Negro affairs seriously both from a personal and intellectual point of view.

The manuscript you have here is almost complete except for the question and answer period. I have left out a paragraph of mine in the introduction which seemed redundant. Some criticism might be made of my choice of the questions and answers. Most were actually more exciting and even hilarious than the ones included here. For example, this exchange between Mr. Wilson and Malcolm X, with a play on the word "spade," a colloquial ghetto term for Negro, had everyone in stitches. Mr. Wilson was responding to a question as to whether a greater proportionate Negro population in a city did manifest itself in actual progress for the group.

MR. WILSON: Your skill at numbers is accurate. . . . If you want to add Cleveland and St. Louis to the list, I would double the argument in spades. . . .   (Laughter)
There was no pun intended. It seems to me that more progress is found in states with a lower proportion of Negroes. . . .

MODERATOR: Malcolm X, would you like to comment?

MALCOLM X: No, I don't think I'd better. I don't know whether to comment on spades or . . . (laughter). But you can see why I believe in separation.

Malcolm X and Martin Kilson also had a very funny exchange. Malcolm X had made the point earlier that middle-class Negroes and Negro intellectuals really distrusted whites as much as the more frank and courageous Negroes he knew. These well-established Negroes told him things in the "closet" which would surprise the whites, he reported. Mr. Kilson, who is a Negro, and Malcolm X had an exchange on just this assessment of the well-established Negro. Malcolm X had just commented on Kilson's speech, and a question had suggested that Mr. Kilson had not really said what he believed. The questioner went on to ask from what vantage point did Mr. Kilson speak.

MR. KILSON: As Malcolm X has suggested to you . . . it's not so easy for a Negro intellectual to discuss these problems, as you may expect. I happen to be an academic and as such I adhere to certain canons of observation and discourse, and of behavior. But [I am] academic who is quite conscious of being a Negro, and rather proud of it. When you ask me from what vantage point I speak, I [must tell you] that I speak from whatever that vantage point is [which permits me] to effectively integrate the difficult position of being both an intellectual and a Negro. I can't satisfy everybody in what I say. Essentially, therefore, I [am] very individualistic about such matters. I seek essentially to satisfy Martin Kilson.   (Applause)

MALCOLM X: May I comment on his comment?   (Laughter)

Well, he is actually proving my point that this middle-class Negro is more frustrated than anybody else.

If you were able to hear one of them in the closet, with none of you around, you would . . . realize how serious this problem is.

You can't be an individual; no black man in this country can be an individual. Dr. Ralph Bunche, an internationally recognized and respected diplomat, was segregated in Atlanta, Georgia.

MR. KILSON: I must comment! Here I think Malcolm is perfectly right. I'm not under the illusion that with respect to white society I can be an individual in the sense that he has in mind. I'm a Negro with respect to white society. But I still argue that an intellectual has certain functions to perform and carries a certain kind of burden. Let me also say in my own self-defense that I am not one who says one thing in public and another thing in the closet.

MALCOLM X: I am happy that I have found a Negro intellectual who will come out of the closet.   (Laughter and applause)

156. The format of this forum was identical with the first Harvard forum. Malcolm X would deliver a speech, there would be re-

buttal by an opposing speaker, an exchange of views between the main speakers would follow, and finally questions would be taken from the floor. The decision what to exclude and change in these speeches was very difficult. Here, it was not someone else and Malcolm X, but, alas, I was the opposing speaker. But I have sought the same clarity of presentation. Malcolm X did not rebutt my speech. I am sure he wished to spare me; for I approached the task of speaking opposite him with considerable apprehension and he surely noticed it.

I have made two changes which should be mentioned. The section of Malcolm X's speech, paragraph ten, was taken from the end of his speech and inserted here. The reason had to do with the general twofold division of the speech. The first part was highly theoretical and the second pragmatic and policy-oriented. The reader will find that Malcolm X discussed the following in the theoretical section: (a) images; (b) images and the Congo; (c) Africa and America from 1939 until 1964. The much shorter policy section was as follows: (a) the Organization of Afro-American Unity; (b) self-defense. The second change was in my speech. My section on Hamlet was originally at the beginning of the speech. Here it is last only to give the literary nature of my analysis in the introductory essay final emphasis.

A Note About the Editor

Archie Epps was born in Lake Charles, Louisiana, in the bayou country. After graduating with honors from Talladega College, in Alabama, he did graduate work in religion at Harvard University, where he gradually developed an interest in Black literature and history. He is now Dean of Students at Harvard College. Mr. Epps, who has worked in civil rights in the Boston area for a number of years, was Boston coordinator of the 1963 March on Washington. He was also a founder of *The Harvard Journal of Negro Affairs*.